GREAT
AMERICAN
BEERS

TWELVE BRANDS THAT BECAME ICONS

BILL YENNE

MBI

First published in 2004 by MBI, an imprint of MBI Publishing Company, Galtier Plaza, Suite 200, 380 Jackson Street, St. Paul, MN 55101-3885 USA

MBI titles are also available at discounts in bulk quantity for industrial or sales-promotional use. For details write to Special Sales Manager at Motorbooks International Wholesalers & Distributors, Galtier Plaza, Suite 200, 380 Jackson Street, St. Paul, MN 55101-3885 USA.

ON THE FRONT COVER: *Photo by John Koharski*

ON THE FRONTISPIECE: Somewhat the worse for wear, this classic Lone Star can from the 1970s rests on a fencepost somewhere in west Texas and invites a cowboy to have a little target practice. *Bill Yenne*

ON THE TITLE PAGE: A myriad of beer labels from 12 brands that became icons. *John Koharski*

ON THE BACK COVER: It is hard to fault the suggestion that the friendliest refreshment that ever bid a guest welcome is a tall, cold bottle of beer. However, the sight of the dog apparently does not please the man with the green tie. Note that the ladies enjoy their Falstaff from Pilsner glasses, while the men drink from bottles. *Author's collection*

Fresh from the trout stream, a perky young lady sits down in this 1961 ad to enjoy a pilsner glass of the beer that "always tastes alive." Schlitz insists that she's looking for a beer with "just the kiss of hops." *Author's collection*

ON THE CONTENTS PAGE: Gleaming chrome, brilliant lucite, and splendid glass await the publican's steady hand. Soon the luminous amber beverage will swirl into the schooner and light the way to happiness for another patient patron. *Bill Yenne*

ISBN 0-7603-1789-5

Printed in China

Contents

Acknowledgments

I thank Mark Ruedich and Tom Allen of North Coast
Brewing (brewers of Today's Acme) for permitting us to
photograph their extensive collection of classic Acme
memorabilia. Thanks are also due to country singer Tracie
Lynn; Tice Nichols of the Miller Brewing Company for
supplying photographs of Girl in the Moon memorabilia;
John Smallshaw for his consultation regarding Falstaff
history; and Walter "Terry" Liebman of Rheingold Brewing,
who kindly shared both memorabilia and recollections.

— Bill Yenne

Introduction

THE BEERS FEATURED IN THIS BOOK are a dozen of the great American beers that inspired true loyalty. These are brands that defined their cities and regions. The people who drank them were more than drinkers, they were fans.

Today's craft beers and microbrews have rich and delicious flavors, as well as exquisite variety. Today's mass-marketed megabrews have enormous advertising budgets, ubiquitous market penetration, and a flavor-neutral taste. The great regional brands discussed in this volume had *soul*.

This is a book about the great brands that became regional, or in some cases, national, icons. These beers had followings akin to those of regional sports teams. The New York–area fans of Rheingold were so loyal that the voter turnout for Miss Rheingold in 1952 and 1956 rivaled that of the presidential elections.

The beers themselves identified with their region, and in turn, the people identified with their regional brews. If you were from St. Paul, Milwaukee, or Austin what else would you want to be seen drinking than "the beer from the Land of Sky Blue Waters," "the Beer That Made Milwaukee Famous," or the "National Beer of Texas"? A big part of the ethos of these brands involved their advertising and slogans. It is hard not to respect "the choicest product of the brewer's art" or "the Champagne of Bottled Beer."

The golden age of the great regional brands was in the three decades after the repeal of Prohibition in 1933. Most of the memorabilia featured in this book comes from these years. Some of the brands have survived, but most are not owned by the original company or brewed at the original brewery.

Of course, we now live in an age when the great brands and the great icons are being rediscovered. Miller Brewing certainly survived, although its legendary Girl in the Moon took a three-decade vacation before she returned to much fanfare in 1997. Acme disappeared abruptly but returned in 1996. Rheingold faded, and the last Miss Rheingold of the twentieth century reigned in 1965. Rheingold returned at the turn of this century, however, and the first Miss Rheingold of the new century was crowned in 2003.

This is a book that takes us back to that golden age of regional brands and regional loyalty. It's about an era when you could walk into just about any bar in Minnesota and watch the Hamm's motion sign as it panned across the lake to the canoe resting on the shore or into any bar in the Northwest and watch the endless flow of the Olympia waterfall. Those who remember these signs will recall the Olympia slogan that assured us that "It's the water!" Of course, it was much more than that. It was the *beer*.

CHAPTER 1

Acme

The Acme Maiden, in her distinctly German setting, appeared on labels almost from the beginning of the Acme brand in 1907. Although her background and costume changed, she remained the Acme icon as the brand went through numerous ownership changes. In this rare Prohibition-era label, the wording assures us that the beverage contains less than a half-percent of alcohol by volume. *ACME COLLECTION, NORTH COAST BREWING COMPANY*

T HE NAME SAYS IT ALL. Webster defines *acme* as "the point of utmost attainment." During the middle of the twentieth century, Acme rose to prominence as the leading brand of beer brewed in California. This ascent coincided with the Golden State's growth as the most populous and economically powerful state in the United States.

The National Brewery, which was founded in 1861 by John Glueck and Charles Hansen at Fulton and Webster streets in San Francisco, was the forerunner of the brewing company that emerged as Acme after Prohibition. The room on the top floor with the louvered windows held open fermenting tanks. AUTHOR COLLECTION

During the 1920s, the term light beer meant something entirely different than it has since 1975. It may have been served in a chilled pilsner glass; light beer was really light in color. The use of clear, rather than brown, glass for the packaging underscored the fact. Until about 1912, clear glass was the standard for beer bottles. ACME COLLECTION, NORTH COAST BREWING COMPANY

This Acme Bock label, probably from the 1940s, uses the familiar Acme script that was used on most Acme labels and point-of-sale materials through the 1950s. A stern and dignified billy goat was the central image on this attractive label. ACME COLLECTION, NORTH COAST BREWING COMPANY

Acme billboards lined the highways and byways throughout California, and the great Acme breweries in San Francisco and Los Angeles pumped out volumes that dwarfed what the other California breweries produced at their plants.

A true testament to the cultural significance of Acme within California is that long after its demise, two modern craft breweries took turns to revive the brand name.

To trace the thread of Acme's history back in time, it begins with the National Brewery, which was established by John Glueck and Charles Hansen at Fulton and Webster streets in San Francisco in 1861. By this time, San Francisco had emerged as the undisputed brewing capital of the Far West, so Glueck and Hansen were in good company.

John Glueck died in 1877, and his widow, Elizabeth Glueck, took his place for three years. In 1880, Hansen became the sole owner of the brewery. The Hansen family was prominent in the company well into the twentieth century.

A second thread of Acme's history can be traced back to 1907, the year after the Great San Francisco Earthquake. In that year, the brand name *Acme* was born across town at the foot of Telegraph Hill with the opening of the Acme Brewing Company at 1401 Sansome Street, on the corner of Greenwich Street.

National Brewery and Acme Brewing came together in 1916 under the same holding-company umbrella. The two formerly independent breweries became the National and Acme plants of the California Brewing Association. It is not known whether the latter was associated with a short-lived brewery that operated in Napa from 1907 to 1909.

The California Brewing Association came into existence at an inopportune time for breweries in the United States. By 1916, the temperance movement was gaining momentum. Two dozen states were already "dry," and in December 1917, the

This pair of quart bottles includes one with an early prewar Acme Bock label and a World War II–vintage package that urges consumers to "Economize with Victory Size." Victory size was a quart, and it saved glass for the war effort. The standard Acme script appears on the Victory label, but the Germanic Fraktur type style is used on the Bock label to underscore its ethnicity. ACME COLLECTION, NORTH COAST BREWING COMPANY

U.S. Congress passed a constitutional amendment to prohibit the manufacture and sale of alcoholic beverages in the United States. The states ratified the 18th Amendment of the Constitution, and Prohibition became law in January 1920. Most of America's breweries were forced to close, but others tried to weather what would be a 13-year nightmare by doing other things. The California Brewing Association's Acme Plant on Sansome became the California Bottling Association, while the National Plant at 722 Fulton Street became the Cereal Products Refining Company.

Many of the brewing companies that tried to stay open during Prohibition brewed "near beer," a beer-like substance that contained less than 1 percent alcohol. Most breweries adopted new brand names for their near beer products. The Acme near beer was unusual because it had the same brand name as its predecessor.

When Prohibition was finally repealed by the 21st Amendment in December 1933, only about half the breweries that had existed beforehand resumed business. However, most of these failed within a few years. The California Brewing Association started brewing Acme beer at Fulton

A whimsical depiction of a billy goat is a common German symbol for bock beer, which is traditionally brewed under the zodiac sign of Capricorn to be consumed in the spring. Many American brewing companies with a German heritage brewed bock beer in the nineteenth century and continued the tradition through the 1930s or 1940s. ACME COLLECTION, NORTH COAST BREWING COMPANY

This post-Prohibition Acme tray was probably used more as a point-of-sale piece in a tavern rather than a tray. Hunting scenes were frequently used in beer advertising through the middle of the twentieth century and weren't out of place in California, where the state's vast San Joaquin Valley abounds with game birds. ACME COLLECTION, NORTH COAST BREWING COMPANY

This close-up of an Acme Bock label from the early 1930s was written partially in German, probably to stress the German origins of the bock style. The phrase at the top proudly proclaims that the product contains only hops and malt, as God intended. The crest, in the three colors of the old German imperial flag, was deleted from the label early on, but the other elements remained and were used off and on until the 1970s. ACME COLLECTION, NORTH COAST BREWING COMPANY

Street, but the Sansome Street plant reopened as the Globe Brewing Company. The latter survived only five years, but Acme burgeoned into a California legend.

Acme struck a chord with consumers, and sales mushroomed. Much of this was in southern California, so the company constructed a new brewery at 2080 East 49th Street in Los Angeles. It opened for business in 1935 and the southern California operation formally did business as the Acme Brewing Company. The San Francisco activity was officially named Acme Breweries until 1943, when the California Brewing Association name was readopted. The Acme brand name continued to be used on the products brewed at both locations.

Meanwhile, an important sister company emerged as the key to Acme's success. The Bohemian Distributing Company was based on a partnership formed in June 1921 between an energetic young beverage salesman named Frank Vitale and J. S. Foto, who operated a small retail beverage store in Los Angeles. A year later, the two partners purchased 50 cases of Acme near beer. This initial transaction evolved into an association with the two Acme breweries that was key to the brand becoming the de facto state beer of California. The Bohemian Distributing Company was the tail that wagged the Acme dog throughout the decades of the brand's rise.

In addition to the San Francisco and Los Angeles distribution centers, Foto and Vitale opened branches in Burbank, Long Beach,

This rare California Brewing Association label dates from the 1933–1936 period and confirms that the company kept the old nineteenth-century brand name alive in the San Francisco and Los Angeles markets, even as Acme was being brewed and sold in both cities. Acme, rather than National, however, became the "National Beer of California." ACME COLLECTION, NORTH COAST BREWING COMPANY

The flagship Acme product was the bottom-fermented Acme Beer, with Acme Bock (a darker lager) a close second. The brewery produced this top-fermented product, but it was probably a small proportion of the company's output. From the label, it seems that Englishtown Ale was probably available only in northern California. The brewery also produced Big Dog Ale and Bull Dog Stout. ACME COLLECTION, NORTH COAST BREWING COMPANY

J. S. Foto, president of the Bohemian Distributing Company of Los Angeles, and Karl Schuster, the San Francisco–based president of Acme Breweries, look uncomfortable as they are interrupted from their shrimp cocktails in 1943. ACME COLLECTION, NORTH COAST BREWING COMPANY

Situated on the wall of a sun-soaked California beer garden, this large Acme point-of-sale piece conjures up memories of the state's early history with a pair of vaqueros on horseback. Molded in the shape of a beer stein, it dates from the heyday of the Acme brand in the mid-twentieth century.
ACME COLLECTION, NORTH COAST BREWING COMPANY

The glass-and-concrete Acme brewery was completed in 1942 on the site of the old National Brewery in San Francisco and was described by architects as one of the world's most beautiful industrial buildings. When this picture was taken on the facility's opening day, the California Brewing Association, owners of the Acme brand, was the largest brewer in California and had plants in San Francisco and Los Angeles.
AUTHOR COLLECTION

San Bernardino, San Diego, Santa Monica, and Bakersfield. Having solidified the California market for Acme during the 1930s, Bohemian expanded its distribution into southern Nevada, Arizona, New Mexico, and western Texas.

In February 1940, Bohemian opened an office and warehouse building adjacent to the Acme plant in Los Angeles. The combined plants comprised five acres. By the 1940s, southern California was the center of gravity for the Acme brand. Karl F. Schuster, Acme's president, remained in San Francisco, but J. S. Foto and Frank Vitale ran operations for both companies from their office in Los Angeles. In addition to being Bohemian's president, Foto was Acme's vice president, and Frank Vitale served as treasurer for both Los Angeles operations.

When the United States entered World War II, Acme was a leading supplier of beer to troops operating in the Pacific Theater. For the home market, Acme encouraged sales of its Victory Size quart bottles with the slogan "Do Your Part—Buy the Quart." The idea was that packaging beer in the larger container conserved the metal necessary for caps, and metal was vital to the war effort.

"Quest for Fortune," original oil painting by Claude Buck

Out of California come reports of
a rare treat in beer...

To every corner of America...the hundreds of thousands of men and women in the Armed Forces and civilians who were on the West Coast during wartime have carried word about a truly great beer brewed in California. They miss its distinctive light quality...its satisfying refreshment.

No wonder...for it was Acme that set the beer pace for America after Repeal...by brewing the first light, dry beer. Acme quickly became the West's best seller. In proportion to California population served, Acme enjoys a greater popularity than any other major brand in the country.

When our breweries are enlarged, we hope to be able to supply those who came West and "discovered" Acme. Meantime, if you wish to enjoy Acme Beer, remember that it affords another reason for planning a return visit to the Pacific Coast!

ACME BREWERIES — San Francisco · Los Angeles

Fine Beers *Since 1860*

Entitled "Quest for Fortune," the Claude Buck painting on this classic World War II–era Acme ad contained many icons from California's early history. The wagon wheel of the pioneers, a shawl, and a tambourine represent the Spanish period; a gun and spurs represent the cowboys; and a gold pan and pick symbolize the 49ers. In the center, the Acme stein includes the two vaqueros, or perhaps they are John C. Fremont's troops arriving to foment the Bear Flag Revolt that led to California's declaration of independence from Mexico in 1846. ACME COLLECTION, NORTH COAST BREWING COMPANY

This vintage Acme tap handle is a reminder of the golden age of Acme draft. The slogan indicates to the bartender that Acme was the favorite, and he didn't need to look any farther to satisfy his patrons. ACME COLLECTION, NORTH COAST BREWING COMPANY

To meet wartime demand, both breweries underwent major upgrades. The new Acme Brewery in Los Angeles was dedicated in June 1943. In San Francisco, Acme's expansion plans included a new brewing plant near the site of the old National Brewery in San Francisco. Architects described this new edifice as "one of the world's most beautiful industrial buildings."

The building was designed by architect William G. Merchant. Born in Healdsburg, in California's Napa County, he lived most of his life in San Francisco. He was licensed in 1920 and worked in the office of the legendary Bernard Maybeck, where he was assistant designer of the Palace of Fine Arts at the Panama-Pacific International Exposition while still in school. When he branched out on his own, he received a number of important commissions for industrial buildings for the Pacific Gas and Electric Company, and he

This cover girl from the official 1943 employee magazine is dressed for a formal affair. It's nice to see a stylish young lady enjoying a glass of cool, clear lager. ACME COLLECTION, NORTH COAST BREWING COMPANY

This is a lineup of Acme beer trucks at the Bohemian Distributing Company in Los Angeles. In this early 1940s photograph, both beer (lager) and ale are promoted on the sides of the trucks. Bohemian had extensive distribution in California, southern Nevada, Arizona, New Mexico, and western Texas. The company maintained a symbiotic operational relationship with Acme. ACME COLLECTION, NORTH COAST BREWING COMPANY

was the architect for three structures at the Golden Gate International Exposition in 1939. After he designed the Acme Brewery, he went on to work on the San Francisco World Trade Center and buildings at San Francisco State University.

When World War II ended, the California economy emerged as the largest and perhaps the most robust in the nation. By the 1950s, the entire country was in the midst of an economic boom that was unprecedented in world history. Against this backdrop, Acme flourished.

Thanks to clever advertising campaigns, Acme literally became the "talk of the town." One such case in point was the legendary "Do YOU Do It?" ad blitz of 1950. Billboards around San Francisco were plastered with slogans claiming that "Outfielders do it," "Left fielders do it," "Fly casters do it," and "Welders do it." Eventually, the billboards claimed

that everyone from acrobats to *die Besten Braumeisters* (the best brewmasters) were doing "it."

The campaign was a take-off on Cole Porter's song "Let's Do It, Let's Fall in Love," which tells us that "birds do it, bees do it, even educated fleas do it." However, where Porter clearly stated that "it" was "falling in love," for the Acme campaign, "it" was drinking Acme beer. Acme played the double entendre game that is loved by advertising agencies.

More than 200 billboards were pressed into service for the campaign, and thousands of lapel buttons were distributed with the legend "Do YOU Do It?" Airplanes with flashing neon signs claimed that "Dracula does it," and 5,000 sets of trick cards went out that said "Magicians do it."

The campaign raised a few eyebrows when fielders and welders were doing "it," but when the billboards went up with the phrase "Telephone girls do it," the buzz around San Francisco became a roar. Executives at the Pacific Telephone and Telegraph Company bristled at the presumption that their female employees were doing either the "it" implied by Acme's double entendre or what was explicitly suggested by Cole Porter.

The columnists at San Francisco's daily papers chattered about the telephone girls for weeks. Bob de Roos said, "The telephone company executives—who regard the ladies in their employ as sacred charges—writhe and groan, particularly when one billboard was pasted upside down, which seemed to make everything that much worse."

The *San Francisco Chronicle*'s legendary Herb Caen put it into perspective when he wryly observed, "The big brass of the phone company and the phone workers' union are baring their fangs at a certain San Francisco beer company for advertising brightly around town: 'Telephone Girls Do It!' All the ad means, natchilly, is that phone goils drink that certain brand of beer. Dear, oh dear."

Ultimately, Acme removed the telephone girl billboards, but the campaign worked. Even against the backdrop of increased competition, Acme had grabbed a 60 percent market share. A new surge of buttons claimed that Acme was preferred six to four.

The 1950s promised great things for consumer products companies. The expanding economy made the road ahead look like clear sailing. However, regional brewers everywhere needed to keep an eye

As the company faded in 1958, the two Acme breweries in San Francisco and Los Angeles ceased brewing Acme. The brand was licensed out and brewed by Blitz-Weinhard of Portland well into the 1970s, however. The 1950s label design of the independent Acme's final days was rejected in favor of the Acme Maiden and her Germanic beer garden setting. ACME COLLECTION, NORTH COAST BREWING COMPANY

This grouping shows the three iterations of the Acme brand after the original Acme breweries ceased production. From left to right, we see the Blitz-Weinhard packaging of the 1970s, the Xcelsior Brewing Company label from the 1980s, and the North Coast Brewing Company label from the 1990s. In each case, the label designer retained the image of the Acme Maiden. ACME COLLECTION, NORTH COAST BREWING COMPANY

on their rear-view mirrors. The national breweries, which had hardly been a factor before World War II, were gaining faster than anyone imagined.

Until the 1950s, brands such as Acme and Lucky Lager owned the California market, but the national giants smelled money in the exploding California economy. Falstaff went into northern California in 1952 and acquired a brewery in San Jose. Pabst arrived in 1953 and acquired the Eastside Brewery on North Main Street in Los Angeles. Eastside dated back to 1897 and also did business as the Los Angeles Brewing Company and the Mission Brewing Company.

Meanwhile, the rapidly growing San Fernando Valley, immediately north of Los Angeles, was emerging as the archetypical postwar American suburban landscape. The two largest brewing companies in the United States went into this area. Both Schlitz and Anheuser-Busch opened new brewing plants in "The Valley" in 1954.

Acme's fortunes declined precipitously. In 1954, as the giants opened their doors, Acme went on the block. The company, along with the San Francisco and Los Angeles breweries, was acquired by Liebmann Breweries of New York. The idea was to brew its famous Rheingold brand on the West Coast. This venture ended four years later. Liebmann pulled out of the Golden State and sold the Los Angeles brewery to the Theodore Hamm Company in 1958.

The nearly new San Francisco brewery, which had been heralded in 1942 as "one of the world's most beautiful industrial buildings," was closed in 1958. It was later demolished for an off-ramp for San Francisco's Central Freeway. No

trace of the freeway remains today. It was completely demolished by 2003. The Los Angeles brewery brewed Hamm's until 1972, when it was closed forever.

The Acme brand name, however, did not die. Blitz-Weinhard of Portland, Oregon, continued to brew small quantities for the California market through the 1970s. After Blitz gave up the trademark, it faded back into obscurity until it was briefly revived in 1987 by Xcelsior Brewing, a microbrewery in Santa Rosa. Xcelsior folded in 1989, and once again, Acme faded away and was recalled only by a handful of nostalgic fans. Among the latter were Mark Ruedrich and Tom Allen, proprietors of the North Coast Brewing Company, a microbrewery born in 1988 on California's Mendocino County coast. Not only were they Acme fans and Acme memorabilia collectors, they owned a brewery. In

This gold foil label touting the brand's availability at the Golden Gate International Exposition in 1939 is another rare bit of Acme ephemera. The fair celebrated the recent completion of the San Francisco– Oakland Bay Bridge, which appears on the label. Treasure Island was a man-made island created for the fair and became a naval base during World War II and remained one for 50 years. ACME COLLECTION, NORTH COAST BREWING COMPANY

This ad was designed in 1950 to be used in supermarket trade publications in California. Joseph Belli, who had sold Acme in his family's San Francisco market since 1936, declared that canned Acme was not only his bestseller but the best beer he had to offer. The 1950 can design featured a full-size illustration of beer in a glass and a redesigned logo with a modernized A. ACME COLLECTION, NORTH COAST BREWING COMPANY

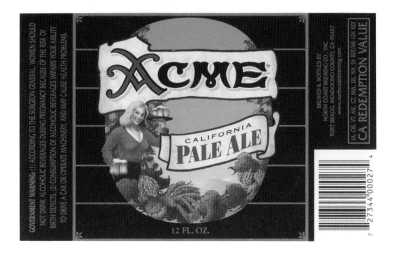

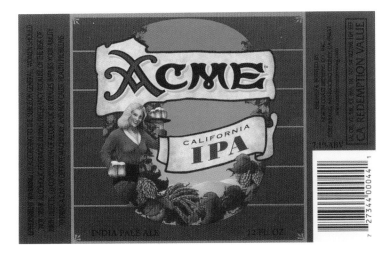

1996 they added Acme to a product line that was headed by their popular Red Seal Ale. At press time, North Coast had three Acme products back in distribution—Acme Brown Ale, Acme California Pale Ale, and Acme India Pale Ale. The Brown won a silver medal at the 1998 World Beer Championships in Chicago, the California Pale won one in 2000, and all three earned silver medals in 2001.

Once again, Californians could ask, "Do YOU Do It?"

This photograph of an Acme point-of-sale piece, date-stamped May 19, 1941, shows that Acme's flagship product was available in cans, at least in northern California, by the early 1940s. Although canned beer first appeared in the mid-1930s, it was much less common than bottled beer throughout the United States until after World War II. ACME COLLECTION, NORTH COAST BREWING COMPANY

North Coast Brewing Company revived the Acme brand for three ale products. Their label design features the classic logotype, but the costume and hairstyle of the Maiden were updated. She has also exchanged the traditional central European porcelain mugs for glassware. ACME COLLECTION, NORTH COAST BREWING COMPANY

Ballantine

T HE AMERICAN brewing tradition and the style of beer most enjoyed by Americans underwent a profound change in the 1840s with the arrival of lager beer from Germany. Americans embraced the new beverage, and their tastes quickly shifted away from their English roots to adopt this bright, crisp, bottom-fermented newcomer. The best-selling American beer brands for the next 140 years were lagers that were first brewed after 1840.

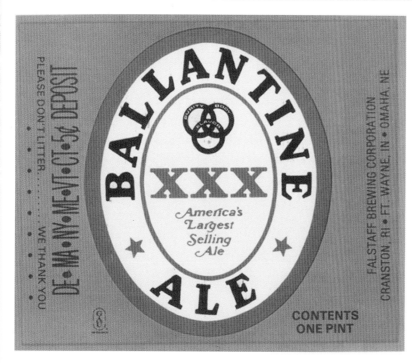

When the Falstaff Brewing Company acquired the Ballantine brand and moved production to Cranston, Rhode Island, in 1972, only the fine print indicated that there had been a change. The three rings and the XXX were still there, as was the assertion that Ballantine was still America's largest-selling ale. In 1972, there was little ale brewed in the United States. AUTHOR COLLECTION

A major exception to this rule was Ballantine, where the old top-fermented ale tradition was perpetuated.

Peter Ballantine was born in November 1791 and grew up in Ayr on the shores of Scotland's Firth of Clyde. He immigrated to America in 1820 and settled in Albany, New York. After working as a brewer for more than a decade, he took over the Robert Dunlop brewery, which was then located on the east side of Broadway above Quackenbush Street. Dunlop started the company in 1806 and Ballantine acquired it in 1833.

In 1840, Ballantine relocated his operations to Newark, New Jersey, to be closer to the rapidly growing market in New York City. Here, he joined forces with Erastus Patterson and took over the brewery that had recently been acquired by Thain and Collins. Founded by General John Cumming in 1805, the brewery operated as the Morton Brothers Brewery between 1832 and 1838.

Peter Ballantine became the sole proprietor of the brewery in 1847. A decade later, the company became P. Ballantine and Sons as the younger members of the family were incorporated into the management of the firm.

The stock in trade at Ballantine during these years was the distinctly

America's Largest Selling Ale

The inscription on the bottle dates this airbrushed illustration to 1942 or shortly thereafter. The label carries Peter Ballantine's three rings of purity, body, and flavor. The brewery at Newark is noted, as is Ballantine's Midtown Manhattan office at 295 Madison Avenue. AUTHOR COLLECTION

THE FAMOUS KING COLE ROOM, AT NEW YORK'S ST. REGIS HOTEL...

Where hospitality is a fine art

IT'S BALLANTINE *Ale* 4 TO 1

P. BALLANTINE & SONS, NEWARK, N.J.

EXOTIC TRADER VIC'S in San Francisco . . . The green bottles so pleasantly in evidence at all the finer places are an invitation to discover Ballantine—the wonderfully different ale. Specially brewed for the American taste, it's America's favorite ale by 4 to 1!

BROADMOOR HOTEL, delightful year-round resort in Colorado Springs. Guests are served one of the world's great drinks . . . Ballantine Ale . . . light as a fine beer but with the time-honored flavor and goodness characteristic of a great ale. Pedigreed yeasts, top-fermentation, dry-hopping bring you this different ale. Next time, call for Ballantine Ale. Expect and *get* something wonderfully different!

24   BALLANTINE THE LIGHT ALE MILLIONS PREFER TO BEER

English style known as India Pale Ale. It had originally been created by the brewers at Burton-upon-Trent in England for export to British colonials living in India. Though pale in color, it was highly hopped because the hops were a preservative on the long trip to India. For this reason, Ballantine claimed his India Pale Ale was aged for a year in wooden barrels, just like the beer of the same style as it made its way to India. Certainly, the conditions in Newark were better for the beer than those on the high seas.

In 1879, the company acquired a second brewery in Newark from the Schalk Brothers, who had begun brewing in 1852. While ale was being brewed at the original Front Street campus, the new facility, situated in the area bounded by Freeman, Christie, Oxford, East Ferry, and Bowery streets, continued as a lager brewery as it had been under the Schalks.

PREPARING THE THANKSGIVING FEAST, painted for Ballantine Beer by Lucile Corcos

Thanksgiving Day at last is here . . .
The family's come from far and near.

The kitchen's smelling mighty nice;
And Dad's got Ballantine on ice.

That's the beer we like the best . . .
Deep-brewed to meet the "icebox test."

We chill the bottles thoroughly . . .
Flavor that chill can't kill, you see!

BALLANTINE (BEER)

Since 1840

_with the Flavor that chill can't kill !

P. Ballantine & Sons, Newark, N. J.

It's always winter in your refrigerator

...that's why Ballantine Beer is brewed for

Flavor that chill can't kill

Ballantine Beer is *deep-brewed* from the world's choicest grains and hops for fine, full flavor that chill can't kill. Serve it as cold as you like; every glass just brims with flavor.

SINCE 1840

BALLANTINE BEER

P. Ballantine & Sons, Newark, N. J.

Ballantine Ale was distinguished by the green glass and green label packaging, while the beer, or lager, was color-coded with brown. The glass is a pilsner rather than a tulip-shape. New England figures were prominently featured in the work produced on Madison Avenue in those days.
AUTHOR COLLECTION

Members of the Schalk family remained active in the brewing business around Newark until the early twentieth century.

Ballantine was the second largest brewing company in the New York City metropolitan area and the sixth largest nationally in the early 1880s. By this time, the original Ballantine plant grew to 12 acres bounded by Front, Fulton, and Rector streets and the Passaic River. The annual output of 106,000 barrels at the beginning of the 1880s expanded to half a million in a decade. It is probably not an exaggeration to say that P. Ballantine and Sons was, at its peak, the largest ale brewery that had existed in the United States during the nineteenth century.

With this major expansion, Peter Ballantine inaugurated his legendary trademark. As the story is told, Ballantine had observed three rings left on a table by a wet beer glass. In those three rings of beer, Ballantine saw a graphically pleasing logo. He decided that these three interlocking rings stood for the three principles that were most important to him in his product. He named the three rings "purity, strength, and flavor." Beginning in 1879, the three-ring logo appeared on Ballantine packaging and advertising for more than a century.

Peter Ballantine became one of Newark's leading citizens and lived in a sprawling mansion on Washington Park that was designed by notable architect George Edward Harny. The oldest of the Ballantine sons, Peter H. Ballantine, died in 1882, from illness after a trip abroad. The elder Peter Ballantine passed away soon after, in January 1883, at the age of 91. Thereafter, the reins of company management passed to son John Herbert Ballantine, and then to son Robert Ballantine.

After the 18th Amendment inflicted the dark era of Prohibition upon America in 1920, Ballantine underwent an abrupt consolidation. The huge brewing plant on Front Street, where Peter Ballantine first brewed ale eight decades before, was closed. The former Schalk brewery on Freeman Street kept the company alive and manufactured malt syrup. Gradually many of the family members who would have joined the company if not for Prohibition drifted away to pursue other interests.

When Prohibition finally ended in 1933, the family was ready to sell. It had been one century since Peter Ballantine had first gone into business. Ironically, the new owners of the nineteenth century's last great English-style brewery in America were German. Otto and Carl W. Badenhausen had made their fortune selling brewery supplies in South America and were ready to start brewing themselves. The brothers did pay their respects to Ballantine's heritage by importing a Scottish brewmaster.

Chapter two of the Ballantine story saw the company come back to prominence both nationally and regionally. By 1940, the company was in the top six nationally, with three of the six being in the New York City area—Ballantine, Ruppert, and Schaeffer. Carl W. Badenhausen had become a respected member of the industry and was named chairman of the United Brewers Industrial Foundation.

During the decade after Prohibition, the new Ballantine had operated as a single-site brewery, but in 1943, the company expanded and acquired what was literally "the brewery next door." This brewery dated from 1866 and was founded by Charles Kolb. It became the Christian Feigenspan Brewery in 1875 and had been famous during the 1930s for its Munich and Pride of Newark brands. This facility operated as Ballantine Plant Two until 1948, when it was closed permanently.

Despite this closing, Ballantine continued to grow. By 1950, the company had an annual output of 4.4 million barrels and was the third largest brewing company in the United States, behind Anheuser-Busch and Schlitz. Its products included both the long-standing India Pale Ale and the Ballantine XXX lager.

Perhaps more significant than the national standing was that Ballantine was number one in the New York City area. This was underscored by the fact that Ballantine sponsored the New York Yankees, the baseball team that rival brewery tycoon Colonel Jacob Ruppert had owned and made legendary between 1915 and 1939. Throughout the 1940s and 1950s, Yankees radio announcer Mel Allen referred to home runs hit at Yankee Stadium as "Ballantine Blasts." Colonel Ruppert must have rolled over in his grave.

Ballantine became such a part of life in America's media capital that even literary figures found it natural to mention the brand. Frank Sinatra mentioned it on stage and John Steinbeck alluded to Ballantine in prose.

"I would rather have a bottle of Ballantine Ale than any other drink after fighting a really big fish," wrote Ernest Hemingway in a rare product endorsement. "We keep it iced in the bait box with chunks of ice packed around it. And you ought to taste it on a hot day when you have worked a big marlin fast because there were sharks after him."

For Ballantine itself, there were sharks in the water: changing times and tastes. A new paradigm was brewing in this business of brewing and distributing beer. After World War II, the Midwest brewers, specifically Anheuser-Busch, Schlitz, Miller, and Pabst, decided to map national strategies. The big brewers in the New York City metropolitan area (Ballantine, Ruppert, and Schaeffer) chose not to.

A skilled cowboy can be a magician with a lasso, although creating three identical circles is a feat worth celebrating with a cold glass of Ballantine Ale. The cowboy made Ballantine seem to be an "Out West" product, despite the fact that the marketing base was within an hour's drive of New York City.
AUTHOR COLLECTION

One ring for **purity**

a second for **body**

a third for **flavor**

Nothing says Valentine's Day like a glass of pale ale. As this clever girl created her card, she recreated the three rings. Peter Ballantine would have had a good chuckle.
AUTHOR COLLECTION

PURITY BODY FLAVOR

To my BALLANTINE

America's largest selling Ale

P. Ballantine & Sons, Newark, N. J

He's pleased with her narrow waist, and she's pleased that he's pleased, but her body language says that he'd better not covet her bottle of Ballantine lager. By the late 1950s, nearly two decades before the light beer marketing push of the late 1970s, the notion was alive that reduced-calorie beer satisfied both the American taste and the American figure. AUTHOR COLLECTION

Brewed to the American taste . . . to the American figure

Ballantine <u>Beer</u> watches your belt-line
...with fewer calories than any other leading beer

Nearly all beers are lower in calories than they used to be. They're all starch-free—and none has more than a negligible trace of sugar.

But . . . if you're counting up your calorie quota, your beer is definitely Ballantine Beer. Independent laboratory tests have shown that it has fewer calories than any other leading beer.

Ballantine, you know, not only watches your belt-line. Ballantine Beer is brewed to the American taste as well as to the American figure.

Ballantine Beer is the product of 114 years of brewing experience. Brewed from nature's finest barley malt and hops, it has the same full flavor and fine character that have made it one of America's largest selling beers.

Next time, ask the man for Ballantine Beer—the low-calorie beer with the flavor that chill can't kill!

P. Ballantine & Sons, Newark, N. J.

"m-m-m, the wonderful flavor that chill can't kill!"

At the time, this seemed to be the appropriate strategy. They were in the biggest beer market in America and among America's largest brewers.

In 1960, Ballantine slipped from third place nationally to sixth, but by 1971, sales had slumped so badly that the company closed the great brewery on Freeman Street. One hundred and thirty-one years after Peter Ballantine first brewed in the city, the last bottle of Ballantine brewed in Newark came off the line and the facility ceased to be a brewery. The sale of the company and trademarks to the Falstaff Brewing Company was concluded in 1972, and production moved to the former Narragansett Brewery in Cranston, Rhode Island. The Narragansett Brewing Company was established in 1890 and had been acquired by Falstaff in 1965.

Because of their great regional legacies, Falstaff wisely chose to keep both the Narragansett and Ballantine brand names alive, and they continued to market the brands to their former constituencies.

In 1975, when the Pabst Brewing Company bought Falstaff, Ballantine production was moved from the Northeast to a brewery in Fort Wayne, Indiana, that Falstaff had acquired from Berghoff Brewing in 1954. This plant operated until 1991, but Ballantine continued to be brewed in small quantities at other Pabst facilities around the United States both before and after that date.

Today, Peter Ballantine's former home in Newark is the last of the great mansions surrounding Washington Park that once housed the city's aristocracy. Now the Newark Museum, it serves as a showcase of period furniture and decorative arts that are reminders of another Newark from long ago. Beer is rarely quaffed under its roof these days.

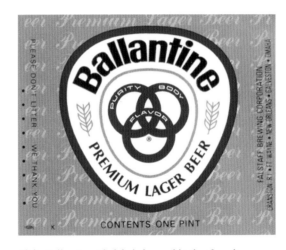

If the Ballantine Ale label changed little after the Falstaff acquisition, the lager label did. What had been "Extra Fine Beer" was now "Premium Lager Beer." AUTHOR COLLECTION

In addition to packaging the pint bottles at Cranston, Falstaff also put Ballantine lager in 11-ounce bottles. This label dated prior to 1977 when Falstaff withdrew from its flagship brewery in St. Louis. AUTHOR COLLECTION

Gansett was the greatest brewery from the smallest state. Founded in 1890 on Depot Avenue in Cranston, just south of Providence, Rhode Island, the brewery became a staple of New England culture, and even sponsored the Boston Red Sox. The phrase, "Hi ya neighbor, have a Gansett," was a popular idiom for most of the twentieth century. Although it was much smaller than Ballantine at its peak, Gansett hosted the Newark native during its final days. AUTHOR COLLECTION

CHAPTER 3

Falstaff

SIR JOHN FALSTAFF was such an engaging and charismatic character that Her Majesty Elizabeth I asked for him by name. Introduced by William Shakespeare as the archetypical "jolly sidekick" in *Henry VI*, Falstaff is regarded as one of the Bard's best-loved creations without a title role. Queen Elizabeth loved him so much that she asked for more. Shakespeare obliged and cast him in a leading role in *The Merry Wives of Windsor*.

Since 1870

FALSTAFF
Beer

12 FL. OZ. (355 ml)

FALSTAFF BREWING CORPORATION
CRANSTON, RI • FT. WAYNE, IN • OMAHA, NE

*The Choicest Product Of
The Brewer's Art.*

This is one of the last Falstaff bottle labels and dates from between 1975, when the flagship St. Louis brewery was closed, and 1984, when S&P padlocked the gate at the old Narragansett Brewery in Rhode Island. *AUTHOR COLLECTION*

He appeared in three plays and was mentioned in a fourth. Genial but generous, Sir John was a knight errant who was much more comfortable at a pun toss or quaffing ale at the Boar's Head Inn than fighting on the battlefield or tournament.

Falstaff would have been right at home with the men who made his a household name in the United States three centuries later. Had William Shakespeare lived in St. Louis, Missouri, in the mid-twentieth century, he might have found the intricate world of its brewing industry worthy of consideration for a historical play. William Lemp and "Papa" Joe Griesedieck, the man who invented Falstaff beer and the man who made it famous respectively, are characters of Shake-spearean dimension. So, too, perhaps, are most of the men associated with St. Louis brewing.

Act 1

The opening scene in the "Tragedy in Five Acts" that is the Falstaff story coincides with the coming of age of St. Louis itself. The first man onto the stage of commercial brewing in St. Louis was Thomas Biddle, who established the Phoenix Brewery around 1825. Within a generation, the Germans arrived and the Phoenix was taken over by Fleischbein and Ketterer in 1835. This set the stage for the grand entrance of the Lemp and Griesedieck families.

Wilhelm Stumpf and George Schneider were among the Germans who opened breweries during the first round of German brewing in St. Louis. Their respective breweries, founded on Decatur Street in 1850 and Carondelet Avenue in

This large bronze bust of Sir John Falstaff, positioned heroically before a manor house, depicts the jolly rogue with a beer stein that bears the crest of the brewery named after him. Throughout much of the twentieth century, tavern patrons asked for his namesake.
BILL YENNE

During the late nineteenth century, William Lemp built his Western Brewery on Cherokee Street into the largest brewery in St. Louis. In 1903, he named a brand of lager after the lovable rascal of Shakespearean drama. AUTHOR COLLECTION

1852, evolved into establishments that played an important part in scenes to come.

Stumpf's brewery employed William Lemp and was later owned by Griesediecks—*twice*. Meanwhile, Schneider's evolved into the most dramatic act in St. Louis brewing history. His company, which came to be known as the Bavarian Brewery from 1856 to 1875, was taken over by Eberhard Anheuser, a salesman to whom the brewery owed money. In the third scene, Anheuser brought his ambitious son-in-law, Adolphus Busch, into the business. The rest is the sort of history that defines St. Louis as the stage for important events in brewing history.

The great breweries of St. Louis, Busch and Falstaff, thrived in part because St. Louis was a small market that was located astride a good rail and river transportation network. Because the market was small, brewers had to broaden their market to succeed.

Before St. Louis, there were the German cities of Stromberg and Eschwege. Today the German city of Stromberg is better known for golf than beer. Scene 1 of the Griesedieck drama begins in 1766, when golf had yet to migrate much farther than Scotland's Firth of Forth. It was in this time and place that the great-grandfather of the Griesedieck brewing family kegged his first beer.

A generation later in Eschwege, where beer is still better known than golf, a teenager named Johann Adam Lemp began his apprenticeship in the brewing industry in about 1810.

In Scene 2 of this act, the action moves to America.

Adam Lemp beat the Griesediecks to St. Louis, although he didn't reach the city until he was 45 years old. With his wife and family in tow, he sailed the Atlantic and arrived in St. Louis by way of Cincinnati in 1838. Lemp started a general store and brewed beer for sale in the back room. Two years later, he started his first full-fledged commercial brewery on South Second Street between Elm and Walnut streets. He was one of the original St. Louis brewers and among the first to brew lager beer, the cold, clear variety created in Bavaria around this point in time. Lager is fermented with a yeast strain that functions at nearly freezing temperatures, in contrast with ale yeast—then the industry standard—which does its work at warmer cellar temperatures.

Lemp became well-known locally in 1845 for using a cave complex south of St. Louis to "lager" or store his products. Lemp harvested large quantities of ice from the Mississippi River in the winter, packed it into his caves, and used it to keep his yeast at the proper temperature.

I've got Falstaff Rhythm, who could ask for anything more? Not only was Falstaff a hit at the bar, but you could also find it on the jukebox. In 1951, Phil Davis and his orchestra got a little help from Len Stokes and the Satisfiers on this 78-rpm recording of the original "Falstaff Rhythm." Sadly, it's hard to find many recordings by the Satisfiers these days. BILL YENNE

DIZZY DEAN'S TROPHY ROOM

Dizzy Dean says: "Make a good time a better time with *Premium Quality Falstaff Beer*"

...AND PAT DEAN (*The Missus*) HAS THE LAST WORD— "I'm just adding a word—to the ladies, this time. More and more of you are serving Falstaff these days...and loving it. Especially when friends drop in to watch Falstaff big league baseball on TV every Saturday, with Dizzy doing the honors. Falstaff makes every such friendly occasion a lot more enjoyable."

THE NATION'S TOAST FROM COAST TO COAST

The Choicest Product of the Brewers' Art

THE FALSTAFF BREWING CORPORATION, ST. LOUIS, MISSOURI
Plants at St. Louis, Mo., Omaha, Neb., New Orleans, La., San Jose, Calif., Fort Wayne, Ind.

What could be better than hanging out with Dizzy Dean in his trophy room and swapping tales while sipping a cold Falstaff? Jerome Herman Dean was the charismatic righthander for the St. Louis Cardinals from 1930 to 1937. He traded the mound for the radio mike in 1941 and made the transition to television a decade later. A Hall of Famer since 1953, he also served as spokesman for the penultimate St. Louis brew.
AUTHOR COLLECTION

Sir John Falstaff made an appearance in this 1953 ad to remind us that his namesake was the "Choicest Product of the Brewers' Art." The fine print reminded us that Falstaff was available from coast to coast, but cautioned us that the supply is still limited. Apparently there had been some distribution problems. Falstaff was on the meteoric rise that took it to third place nationally, but there were going to be some bumps in the road.

AUTHOR COLLECTION

The once-proud Falstaff insignia is still visible on the exterior of the red brick building at the old Falstaff brewery in St. Louis. If you close your eyes, you can almost smell the wort and hear the clatter of brewery horses' hooves on the street.

BILL YENNE

Will he get the can of Falstaff without getting his suede buck wet? On a picnic with three fellows, this young lady can afford to be a bit of a tease, but we hope there will be plenty of burgers and beer when the hijinks are over. In this ad from the late 1950s, we're invited to fill our cooler with cans or one-way bottles. The invention of the no-deposit, no-return bottle was considered an important step toward modernization. The days when you had to pay a deposit and return the bottles to be refilled were gone. Within a generation, the one-way bottle was a symbol of environmental irresponsibility.

AUTHOR COLLECTION

Good Times
are better with
*Light,
Refreshing*
Falstaff

Cool, golden Falstaff tops your good time with good taste. The light, refreshing taste of beer at its premium quality best.

AMERICA'S PREMIUM QUALITY BEER

She looks as though she's having a good time, and she's probably fun to have around, but after a few Falstaffs, we won't want her near the tiller. By the time this ad appeared, Falstaff was riding high, approaching an annual output of five million barrels.
AUTHOR COLLECTION

Act 2

Adam Lemp passed away in 1862, and a year earlier, ownership of the brewery had been transferred to his 25-year-old son, William Jacob Lemp. Before he went to work for his father, young William had been an employee and a partner since 1860 in the Wilhelm Stumpf Brewery.

William, along with his nephew, Charles Brauneck, operated Adam Lemp's brewery as the William J. Lemp and Company Western Brewery until 1864, when William bought his nephew's share. William began a major expansion project of

It is hard to fault the suggestion that "the friendliest refreshment that ever bid a guest welcome" is a tall, cold bottle of beer. However, the sight of the dog apparently does not please the man with the green tie. Note that the women enjoy their Falstaff from pilsner glasses, while the men drink from bottles. AUTHOR COLLECTION

a much larger brewery and storage facility on Cherokee Street near Carondelet Avenue. William's interest in the former Stumpf property apparently ended in 1866, when his name was dropped from the official company name.

Enter the great-grandsons of Johann Heinrich Griesedieck—Anton and Heinrich—in Act 2, Scene 2. As William Lemp built his new Western Brewery, the younger Griesediecks arrived in America. They probably chose St. Louis because, in the 1860s, St. Louis was the "West" and the West was synonymous with opportunity.

Anton and Heinrich Griesedieck both worked in the brewing trade and set the stage for a prominent role for the family. Anton's son, Joseph, later known as "Papa Joe," was

"Barbecue on the Range"

born in 1863 and grew up at the brewery. By 1870, the year that Joe was sent off to the U.S. Brewing Academy in New York City, Anton acquired his first brewery.

In 1879, Joe coincidently acquired the former Wilhelm Stumpf Company, which had gone through a series of name changes and had been relocated to the corner of Buena Vista Street and Shenandoah Avenue. Anton Griesedieck sold out three years later and bought a brewery at 18th and Lafayette. This time, the brewery was the venerable Phoenix.

In the meantime, William Lemp built the Western Brewery into the city's largest, with a place in the top 20 largest breweries nationally. In second place to Lemp's operation was Eberhard Anheuser's Bavarian Brewery, which was soon taken over by Anheuser's son-in-law, Adolphus Busch.

For the remainder of the century, Lemp and Busch were the most powerful men in St. Louis brewing, as well as two of the city's most colorful characters. Their competitiveness led them to be pioneers in such innovations as large-scale bottling, artificial ice-making, and proprietary railroads dedicated to beer distribution. Together, they turned their city into a brewing central that rivaled Milwaukee.

By the end of the century, Lemp exported to Canada, Mexico, Europe, and the Far East. St. Louis–brewed Lemp lager was even sold in Germany, which was a major triumph for an immigrant family.

St. Louis was the land of opportunity, and opportunity came knocking in 1889. The British saw the boundless American appetite for beer as a means to access that opportunity. Well financed with investment capital, a British consortium created large brewing companies by acquiring numerous smaller ones in the same area. First, they went to Milwaukee to merge Pabst, Schlitz, and Blatz into a mega-brewery. Having failed there, they turned to St. Louis. Both William Joseph Lemp and Adolphus Busch, by now the leading figures on the St. Louis scene, turned them down, but the Brits succeeded in consolidating no fewer than 18 breweries into a single entity called the St. Louis Brewing Association. It was one of the biggest regional consolidations of the nineteenth century.

Anton Griesedieck was among those who sold his company to the St. Louis Brewing Association, but this did not bring the curtain down on the Griesediecks. Anton and his brother—who had, by now, Anglicized his name from "Heinrich" to "Henry"—moved to 18th and Gratiot to reopen as the National Brewery. In 1891, Papa Joe Griesedieck took over this facility, which was the base of operations until 1906.

In great theater, the curtain is often brought down on an act with a dramatic, and often tragic, climactic scene. Thus was the case with William J. Lemp.

As the curtain goes up on the final scene of this act, the venerable patriarch is surrounded by the younger, third-generation Lemps. There is Charles, the company treasurer; Louis, the brewery superintendent; and William J. Lemp Jr., the corporate vice president. It is 1903 and they created the legendary brand name. Sir John Falstaff, the lovable rogue of Shakespearean drama, is adopted as the Lemp trademark, and Falstaff beer is born.

Dark tragedy lurks in the wings. Less than a year later, in February 1904, on the eve of the St. Louis World's Fair, William J. Lemp, committed suicide.

Sir John was long forgotten by now, but in the 1970s, Falstaff's ad agency decided to resurrect Papa Joe Griesedieck as a spokesman for the product in the age of the pull tab. The assertion that "this family brews better beer" was probably not taken very well at the home of the Busch family. JOHN SMALLSHAW COLLECTION

Act 3

The third act begins hopefully. William J. Lemp Jr. took over the reins of the company and the Falstaff brand had a major presence at the 1904 World's Fair. Scott Joplin debuted ragtime piano, and Lemp debuted Falstaff beer.

In Scene 2, the Griesediecks took over the lead role in our drama. In 1906, nine breweries united to become the Independent Breweries Company. Papa Joe

What a time for Falstaff.
Crisp. Clean. Robust.
For four generations, good taste has made Falstaff
the choicest product of the brewers' art.® Everywhere.

Falstaff Brewing Corp., St. Louis, Mo.

Bringing along a cooler of Falstaff for one of those warm summer evenings was still "the friendliest refreshment that ever bid a guest welcome." JOHN SMALLSHAW COLLECTION

Griesedieck's National Brewery was one of the nine breweries involved. The creators of this new consortium chose their name to distinguish a group of local companies from St. Louis Brewing Association, which had been formed 17 years before by the hand of the British venture capitalists. Both Lemp and Busch remained independent.

As had been the case with Anton Griesedieck in 1889, Henry Griesedieck sold out to consolidation and struck out on his own. In 1911, five years after the merger, Henry bought the Consumers Brewing Company, one of the nine components out of the Independent Breweries Company. It was not the former Griesedieck National Brewery that he had folded into the Independent Breweries Company in 1906, but the Consumers Brewing Company. This company traced its lineage back to the Wilhelm Stumpf property that had been Lemp-owned between 1860 and 1866 and Griesedieck-owned from 1879 to 1882!

As with Act 2, the curtain goes up on the final scene of Act 3 on the eve of impending tragedy— Prohibition. This act also ends with the venerable patriarch, surrounded by the younger generation. In this case, it is Henry Griesedieck and his sons, Anton, Henry, Raymond, Robert, and Edward. Consumers was renamed the Griesedieck Brothers Brewery Company after Henry Sr. passed away.

Meanwhile, Papa Joe was ready to make his next move. In 1917, even as national Prohibition was a virtual certainty, he acquired the seven-year-old Forest Park Brewing Company on Forest Park Boulevard. He renamed it the Griesedieck Beverage Company and obviously anticipated he wouldn't brew much beer at the site in the immediate future.

Prohibition became law in January 1920 and sent a ripple of despair throughout the brewing industry. Some companies survived the next decade with alternative beverages such as near beer, but most folded. Among the St. Louis giants to tumble was the William J. Lemp Brewing Company. One of the last steps taken by the Lemps before the mighty gates on Cherokee Street were padlocked for the last time was to sell the Falstaff trademark to Papa Joe Griesedieck for $25,000. He promptly renamed the Griesedieck Beverage Company as the Falstaff Brewing

Corporation. As the curtain goes down on Act 3, Papa Joe walked into the gathering darkness virtually penniless, but he carried a golden prize.

Act 4

The curtain rises as the sun comes out from behind the dark cloud of Prohibition. Although it will finally be repealed through enactment of the 21st Amendment in December 1933, emergency permits authorized by the incoming Roosevelt Administration in April 1933 allowed beer production to resume. Permit number one was issued to Papa Joe Griesedieck.

During Prohibition, while Papa Joe whiled away his time smoking hams and producing Falstaff and Hek near beer, his cousins at the Griesedieck Brothers Brewery Company survived by making soft drinks.

Also in 1933, another cousin, Henry L. Griesedieck, crossed the river into Illinois and acquired the Western Brewery in Belleville. Founded in 1851 by Philip Neu and Peter Gintz, the company became the Griesedieck Western Brewery Company, but it will be best known as "Stag," the brand name of the beer that it produced. Griesedieck Western continued as an independent until 1954, when it was acquired by Canada's Carling. In turn, Carling's U.S. operations was acquired by G. Heileman in 1979. The brewery and the Stag brand survived until 1988, when Heileman closed the Belleville facility permanently.

Through the middle decades of the twentieth century, relations between the three beer-brewing branches of the Griesedieck family was marked by intense rivalry. As for Papa Joe Griesedieck, it was his turn to assume the starring role on the St. Louis brewing stage and become a major player. Having grown up watching the effects of the great St. Louis brewery consolidations of 1889 and 1906, Papa Joe saw this strategy

as the road to his own future success. In 1933, just a matter of weeks after he received permit number one, Papa Joe acquired Otto Stifel's Union Brewery on Michigan Avenue and incorporated it into his empire as Falstaff Brewing Corporation Plant Two.

The following year, with two facilities running in St. Louis, Papa Joe looked south to New Orleans, where he acquired the National Brewing Company, which was founded in 1911. In 1937, Papa Joe turned west to Omaha, Nebraska, and purchased a brewery started by Fred Krug in 1859. The two properties both ran the flag of the Falstaff Brewing Company, and Papa Joe became

The catcher is definitely happy to see that the pitcher is drinking his Falstaff from a stubbie. The basis for such packaging being "the one" for lighthearted moments is lost in the folds of double entendre. JOHN SMALLSHAW COLLECTION

For your Light-hearted moments...

THIS IS THE ONE

the first major brewing magnate to operate breweries in three separate states. In a few short years after the repeal of Prohibition, he established Sir John's surname as one of the pre-eminent beer brands in America.

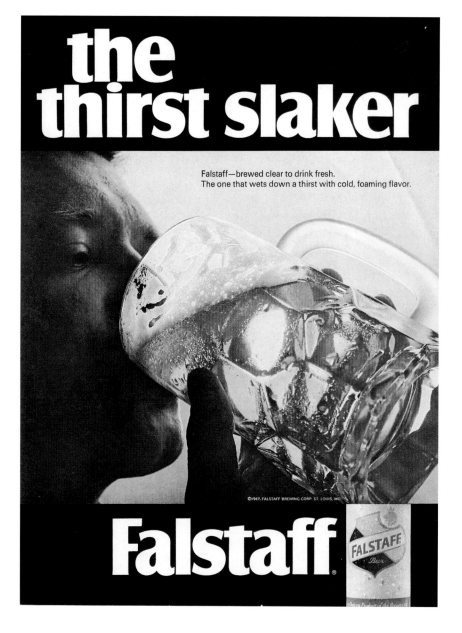

Act 4, Scene 1 ends with Papa Joe at the peak of his prominence; however, his time upon the stage was soon over. On July 14, 1938, three days past his 75th birthday, Papa Joe died. His son, Alvin Griesedieck, took over the Falstaff empire.

More than a decade passed before Alvin resumed building the empire that his father had pursued. His immediate concern at the turn of the decade and through World War II was to fend off competition within the St. Louis market from his cousins, the Griesedieck brothers. Their "GB" beer was being marketed under the nickname "Good Beer." With output exceeding a million barrels annually, the brothers' operations within St. Louis were on par with Anheuser-Busch. In fact, Griesedieck Brothers had an exclusive sponsorship contract for the radio broadcasts of Cardinals baseball games. For a while after the Busch family acquired the Cardinals in 1953, the Griesedieck Brothers continued to pitch its beer in Cardinals broadcasts.

In 1948, with the acquisition of the Columbia Brewery on Madison Street, Alvin Griesedieck showed he was ready to resume a campaign of acquisitions that would have made Papa Joe proud. The Columbia Brewery was founded in 1892 and had been one of the components of the Independent Breweries Company from 1906 to 1919. For the next four years, Falstaff operated three breweries within the city, then Alvin Griesedieck closed the former Union Brewery property on Michigan Avenue in 1952. The savings allowed him to continue a systematic plan for national expansion.

By the early 1950s, California had the fastest-growing economy and population in the nation. Just as St. Louis had been the land of opportunity a century before, all eyes were now on the Golden State. Pabst and Schlitz, the big Milwaukee companies, opened plants in California by the end of 1954, as did Alvin's big cross-town rival, Anheuser-Busch. However, Falstaff beat them all.

In 1952, Alvin Griesedieck purchased the Wieland Brewing Company site in San Jose that had originated in 1856 as Gottfried Krahenberg's Fredericksburg Brewery.

Two years later, with five breweries in four states, Alvin acquired the Bergoff Brewery, which had been a Fort Wayne, Indiana, institution since 1887. In 1956, Alvin Griesedieck looked south into Texas. At that time, the major center of brewing in the Lone Star State was in San Antonio. The city was home to both Pearl and Lone Star beers, so Alvin looked elsewhere and picked two acquisitions at opposite edges of the state. In 1956, the former Mitchell Brewery in El Paso and the Galveston Brewing Company in Galveston became Falstaff breweries.

With eight plants in six states, Alvin Griesedieck now had the largest and most comprehensive national brewery empire in the United States. It was a major accomplishment, but it was overshadowed by the events of 1957. In that year, he finally concluded the ongoing negotiations with his cousin Henry Griesedieck for Falstaff to take over the Griesedieck Brothers Brewery Company. With this, he closed the antiquated Plant One on Forest Park Boulevard and shifted production to more efficient units.

The three decades after the repeal of Prohibition were Falstaff's triumph. In the ten years from 1950 to 1960 alone, Alvin Griesedieck saw Falstaff grow from the seventh-largest brewing company in the United States to number three. He had beat out such industry giants as Ballantine, Schaeffer, Miller, and Pabst. Only Schlitz and Anheuser-Busch were bigger than Falstaff. It was, as the company advertising insisted, "The Choicest Product of the Brewer's Art."

As had been the case with Papa Joe, Alvin would leave the stage at the apogee of his game.

From the 1950s to the 1970s, Falstaff's marketing had gone from positioning it in the nation's best bars and restaurants to suggesting a six-pack should be slammed down while the team still had its first possession of the ball. JOHN SMALLSHAW COLLECTION

Act 5

Act 5 opens with the funeral of Alvin Griesedieck, the only man other than William Shakespeare who did more than Papa Joe to make Falstaff a household name. If Act 4 had been Falstaff's shining hour, then Act 5 was its descent into darkness.

Just as Alvin picked up the baton when Papa Joe left the stage in 1938, Alvin's son, Joseph II, followed Alvin onto stage center in 1961. However, Joseph Griesedieck's tenure would be the antithesis of the glory that his father and grandfather experienced with Falstaff.

In 1965, Joseph Griesedieck II resumed the tactic that had worked so well for his predecessors. Where they had looked mainly to the West and South for expansion opportunities, Joseph II looked to the populous Northeast. In 1965, he

The only beer that always tastes light enough to have another.

The suggestion that Falstaff is the "only beer that always tastes light enough to have another" has to rank among the worst reasons to drink beer. This slogan was coined during the 1970s when the push toward tasteless beers ruined the great heritage of American brewing. In the fashion world, they have a saying that the 1970s was the decade that taste forgot. A similar statement is sadly true of mass market brewing in that era. JOHN SMALLSHAW COLLECTION

bought the Narragansett Brewing Company, the largest brewing company in New England. Narragansett was founded in 1890 at Cranston, Rhode Island, and owned the trademarks of the former Gottfried Krueger Brewing Company, which had existed in Newark, New Jersey, from 1852 to 1961.

Joseph Griesedieck II's first foray into the acquisitions business looked good on paper, and it would have worked out nicely if not for the intervention of the state of Rhode Island. The state was protective of a home-grown business being swallowed by an out-of-state giant and filed antitrust charges against Falstaff.

The battle lines were drawn and the attorneys were called. Falstaff literally went broke defending its final brewery acquisition. To pay legal expenses, Falstaff had to close breweries. Both the El Paso plant and the former Columbia facility in St. Louis were closed in 1967. In 1971, however, Falstaff picked up the former Burgermeister Brewery in San Francisco that had been owned briefly by Schlitz. With this brewery in operation, the one in San Jose was closed in 1973.

In 1972, Falstaff made a second costly attempt to enter the market in the Northeast by acquiring the trademark rights to the Ballantine brands and unsuccessfully attempted to market them.

When the Rhode Island antitrust case was finally settled in the U.S. Supreme Court in 1973, Falstaff had won a victory that bled the company treasury dry. The Griesedieck family made several attempts to find investors but had no success. Finally, in April 1975, they sold controlling interest in the company to Paul Kalmanovitz, a reclusive California tycoon who had recently acquired the General Brewing/Lucky Lager family of breweries through his S&P Holdings company.

Kalmanovitz was known for controlling costs through radical downsizing and promptly closed Falstaff's St. Louis headquarters and laid off hundreds of workers. He then quickly closed

Kalmanovitz left the stage in 1987 after he acquired Pabst and closed its Milwaukee brewery. He died having made far more enemies than friends in the American brewing industry. His holding company survived and did business under the Pabst name. Having taken over a dizzying variety of well-known labels from Lucky Lager to Pearl, the new Pabst acquired Stroh Brewing of Detroit in 1999. Stroh, which had owned Schlitz since 1982, had acquired Heileman in 1996. Heileman already owned such well-known, formerly independent brands as Grain Belt, Lone Star, Rainier, and Blitz-Weinhard. This gave Pabst a portfolio of some of the greatest brand names in American history. The last actual Pabst brewing plant, the former Pearl facility in San Antonio, ceased brewing at the end of 2002. Whatever beers from the Pabst portfolio that are still brewed are all produced under contract by other brewing companies.

The curtain on Falstaff's final scene came down when the Falstaff headquarters in St. Louis closed in 1975. With the passing of the Fort Wayne Brewery in 1991, none of the Falstaff breweries were left in operation.

In 1976, Falstaff undertook one of its last great promotions and created special packaging to celebrate the United States' bicentennial. The schooner was a vintage piece and carried the classic slogan "the Choicest Product of the Brewers' Art." BILL YENNE

Falstaff facilities just as fast as Alvin Griesedieck added them two decades before. One by one, the lights went out on the great archipelago of Falstaff breweries.

The last Falstaff St. Louis plant—ironically the Griesedieck Brothers' facility—closed in 1977. Falstaff's recently acquired San Francisco Brewery was shut down in 1978, followed by the New Orleans facility in 1979, which had been a Falstaff Brewery for 40 years. Galveston was closed in 1981, and Omaha, Papa Joe's first out-of-state acquisition, closed in 1987. The Naragansett Brewery, which Falstaff might have survived without, was gone by 1984.

This porcelain sign is typical of those that promoted "the Choicest Product of the Brewers' Art" at retail venues throughout the Midwest and from coast to coast. DAN AUGUSTINER COLLECTION

This is a classic Hamm's label from the early 1970s, when the only Hamm's brewery outside the Land of Sky Blue Waters was the one near the former Seals Stadium in San Francisco. *AUTHOR COLLECTION*

CHAPTER 4

Hamm's

THROUGHOUT THE history of advertising and packaging, animals have been a popular icon. When it comes to beer, rampant lions growl from labels across Europe. In the nineteenth century, eagles perched upon the marquees and labels of countless breweries. However, when it comes to the history of U.S. brewing companies, no animal ever used can match the immortal Hamm's Bear.

Throughout the middle part of the twentieth century, the Hamm's Bear and his little woodland pals were the ubiquitous symbols of the celebrated beer "from the Land of Sky Blue Waters."

However, before there was a beer from the Land of Sky Blue Waters, there was a brewer who made his way to the Land of Sky Blue Waters.

Theodore Hamm was born in Herbolzheim in the German state of Baden in 1825. He immigrated to the United States and arrived in St. Paul, Minnesota, in 1856. The growing German population of the city supported a number of breweries. In his early days in America, Hamm consumed the products of St. Paul's brewers rather than produced them.

The first commercial brewery in St. Paul was started by Anton Yoerg on South Washington Street between Chestnut and Eagle in 1848. Across the Mississippi River in Minneapolis, John (Johann) Orth started brewing in 1850 at what evolved into Minneapolis Brewing and Malting, producers of the legendary Grain Belt brand that was the chief Minnesota rival for Hamm's.

Another early commercial brewing company in St. Paul was constructed by a man named Andrew Keller in 1860

(left)
By the time these men sipped their Preferred Stock, Hamm's had been the favorite of millions for 81 years. This dated their skiing trip to 1946.
AUTHOR COLLECTION

(right)
After a day of hunting, it's time to clean the shotgun and enjoy a beer. This is part of a series of ads from the late 1940s that featured the striking scratchboard illustration of the "Preferred Stock hand."
AUTHOR COLLECTION

over an artesian spring in the Swede Hollow area near Phalen Creek. Keller later borrowed money from Theodore Hamm, put his brewery up for collateral, and defaulted in 1865. Eventually, Hamm took over the brewery.

Historical records list various names for this establishment under Keller's ownership. Some list it as the Pittsburgh brewery, while others call it the Excelsior Brewery. After Hamm took over, it was known as the Theodore (or Theo) Hamm Brewery or Brewing Company; however, Hamm used the Excelsior brand name for some of his products. Other Hamm brand names included Preferred Stock, New Brew, and Velvet.

In addition to brewing beer, Hamm was a retail purveyor of his products. City directories for the ensuing years list his business as a brewery and summer garden.

When Theodore's son, William, joined his father's company in 1886, the brewery was the second largest in Minnesota and had an annual

This schooner of cold Hamm's displays the Land of Sky Blue Waters slogan and a bottle of Hamm's Preferred Stock beer. The brand was the company's flagship through the mid-1950s. BILL YENNE

The young folks on the patio are overjoyed with the prospect of the Preferred Stock on its way. The beer barrel mugs are definitely late 1940s period pieces.
AUTHOR COLLECTION

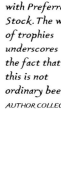

This ad, part of a series illustrated by Charles McBarron in 1947, depicts a thirsty foursome bound for their rendezvous with Preferred Stock. The wall of trophies underscores the fact that this is not ordinary beer.
AUTHOR COLLECTION

The Hamm's brewery near Seals Stadium in San Francisco opened in June 1954 and had one of the greatest outdoor advertising pieces in brewing history on its roof. The 39-foot beer glass had 2,300 feet of yellow and white neon tubing. The glass was "filled and drained" thousands of times over the next 19 years. The Hamm's script on the building was changed to block lettering in 1966. AUTHOR COLLECTION

production of 40,000 barrels. Output was huge compared to the paltry 500 barrels that the facility produced when Theodore Hamm took over two decades earlier. By the first decade of the twentieth century, production topped 700,000 barrels annually. Behind the scenes, the true business genius in the Hamm family was Theodore's wife, Louise. She was the bookkeeper and corporate manager to whom the true credit is due for the fortunes of the Hamm Brewing Company.

When Theodore Hamm died in 1903, William assumed the helm of the company and was joined by his son, William Hamm

This 1949 ad works the Hamm's "Smooth and Mellow" slogan into an eight-part barbecue recipe. It may have been an "old Korean" recipe, but the cattle brand motif on the dishware was strictly western Americana. AUTHOR COLLECTION

In this archetypical rendering of the Hamm's Bear, he proudly delivers a foaming schooner. He was probably the greatest animated animal icon in the history of American brewing. AUTHOR COLLECTION

This Hamm's Preferred Stock coaster featured the original nineteenth-century eagle insignia on one side and a line drawing of the St. Paul brewery on the reverse. It appeared in 1972 when Hamm's briefly reintroduced and test-marketed a second-generation Preferred Stock beer. AUTHOR COLLECTION

Jr. Meanwhile, William Figge, a descendent of Theodore Hamm's first brewmaster, moved into the role of general superintendent and brewmaster of the company.

During the dark years of Prohibition, the Hamm Brewing Company diversified and produced and sold near beer, soft drinks, cigars, and sardines. Digesto Brand malt extract was also on the list and had been marketed toward "nursing mothers" and "tired house-wives" since the early 1900s.

When Prohibition ended, Hamm was back in action. Although the repeal wasn't enacted until the end of 1933, an emergency measure authorized by President Roosevelt permitted the sale of beer beginning at midnight on April 6. Hamm's Beer was brewed, fermented, and bottled by that hour, and the motors of the Hamm's delivery trucks were already running when the clock struck midnight.

Two months later, near-disaster visited the Hamm family. The years of Prohibition had provided an open door

In this 1956 Land of Sky Blue Waters ad, the Hamm's bear was joined by other woodland creatures he shared space with during his early years. Many of them, especially the beaver, were widely used in the 1950s before the bear emerged as the sole animal icon. AUTHOR COLLECTION

This classic Hamm's coaster put the bear in black tie. The slogan "Round after round it goes" was short-lived. *AUTHOR COLLECTION*

In this Hamm's coaster from the company's centennial year, the "crown and trees" logo was used and the definitive rendering of the bear had been standardized. *AUTHOR COLLECTION*

This 1955 ad was a classic view of the Land of Sky Blue Waters with the "Refreshingly yours" slogan in play. Carl Paulson's beautifully airbrushed illustration includes the sunburst label design that was introduced around this time. Preferred Stock had been eliminated in favor of calling the beer Hamm's, although the word **preferred** was retained for several years. *AUTHOR COLLECTION*

In this early version of the Hamm's Bear, possibly from around 1954, his ears were smaller and less defined than the renderings after the early 1960s. *AUTHOR COLLECTION*

for elements of organized crime and allowed gangsters to have a free reign in creating nefarious empires built on a foundation of illicit booze.

One of the most notorious gang leaders of the era was Arizona Donnie Clark Barker, best known simply as Ma Barker. By the 1920s, Ma's gang of bank robbers included her

Yours, at the bewitching hour
...from the land of sky blue waters.

Hamm's!

Make your toast with something just a little bit better. Get acquainted with that wonderful bit of difference that makes Hamm's the most popular beer of all in the area where it is sold.

Discover a special kind of crisp, clean-cut taste, captured in the land of sky blue waters. Just say the word—"Hamm's"—the one and only Hamm's Beer.

Always the same refreshing flavor... glass after glass after glass!

Theo. Hamm Brewing Co., St. Paul, Minn., San Francisco and Los Angeles, Calif.

A young couple toasts the sunset at the bewitching hour in the Land of Sky Blue Waters. This ad dates from between 1958, when the Los Angeles brewery came online, and 1963, when Hamm's opened a plant in Houston. Note that the sunburst label no longer carries the word preferred.
AUTHOR COLLECTION

sons, Herman, Lloyd, Arthur, and Fred, among others. The Barker gang was also affiliated with the notorious Alvin Karpowicz, better known as Creepy Karpis. In 1933, Ma Barker decided to change the gang's direction from bank robbery to kidnapping for ransom.

At about 12:45 p.m. in the afternoon of June 15, 1933, William Hamm Jr. left the brewery offices on East Minnehaha Avenue and started walking toward the Hamm family mansion on Cable Avenue. Two blocks from his office door, Hamm was accosted by Creepy Karpis and Fred Barker, who shoved him into a car. He was taken to a house in Bensonville, Illinois, near Chicago. Demands were made that the Hamm family should pay $100,000 for his return. The payment was made, and three days

This Hamm's menu cover from the mid-1960s features a color photograph of the Land of Sky Blue Waters, instead of an illustration. It is reminiscent of the classic lighted and motion signs the company produced for restaurants and taverns during this period. AUTHOR COLLECTION

Menu

FROM THE LAND OF SKY BLUE WATERS

Hamm's BEER

This series of drawings are rough sketches for Hamm's Bear point-of-sale mobiles to celebrate Christmas.
AUTHOR COLLECTION

Hamm's

From the land of sky blue waters... America's classic premium beer since 1865

Hamm's | Refreshing as the land of sky blue waters

so cool (as the northern breezes)
so fresh (as the rushing streams)
so light...so bright
so smooth...so clear
"that's Hamm's—my kind of beer!"

Freshness...that's Hamm's!

the freshness of the land of sky blue waters

This 1964 ad features text adapted from radio advertising that ran at the time. By now the sunburst yellow label of the 1950s had been superseded by the stylized crown and trees motif. AUTHOR COLLECTION

later William Hamm walked free. A Chicago bootlegger named Roger Touhy was later charged with the kidnapping, but he was acquitted. Ma and Fred Barker were killed by FBI agents in 1935, and Creepy Karpis was arrested on other charges. A one-time "Public Enemy Number One," Karpis later had the distinction of being the longest-serving resident of Alcatraz.

In 1951, the 46-year-old William C. Figge, son of former Hamm's brewmaster William Figge, left his law career and became president of the Theodore Hamm Brewing Company. This event marked a major turning point in the history of the brewery. The expanding postwar American

In 1973, Hamm's traded the cartoon bear for a live one. The bear was a Kodiak named Sasha who was born at the Los Angeles Zoo but was raised in Canada. Sasha's sidekick was animal trainer Earl Hammond. A series of television commercials filmed in northern California debuted in June 1973. The commercials were quite popular, and more commercials were filmed in 1974 near Lake Seagull and Lake Saganaga in Minnesota. AUTHOR COLLECTION

economy afforded numerous opportunities for growing a business. Figge decided to seize the moment and transform Hamm's from a regional favorite into a national brand to be reckoned with.

Figge worked with Ray Mithun of the Campbell-Mithun advertising agency and oversaw the development of the immortal slogan, "from the Land of Sky Blue Waters." Minnesota was promoted as a recreation paradise of "10,000 Lakes," and the two slogans neatly supported one another. The state later honored Figge and named a lake in the Superior National Forest after him.

Having created the image of a "land," Campbell-Mithun created characters to inhabit the land. Nobody recalls for sure who came up with the idea of an animated bear to promote Hamm's Beer. Albert Whitman at Campbell-Mithun is

This strange cutaway illustration from 1967 explained that your mug of Hamm's contained not just lager, but the Land of Sky Blue Waters itself! Those sky blue waters that were best for brewing were now a registered trademark.
AUTHOR COLLECTION

Hamm's inside story: water best for brewing

To cut a long story short—this beer was born and raised in big water country. Clean, fresh country. Brilliantly pure water. The best brewing water nature provides. Which helps account for Hamm's

©1967 Theo. Hamm Brewing Co., plants in St. Paul, Minn., San Francisco, Los Angeles

crisp, clean-cut taste and refreshing feel. The smoothness is aged in. The result is beer that never stops refreshing you. Round after round. Glass after glass. Say, why not open one up yourself, right now?

From the land of sky blue waters—comes the water best for brewing

A smiling Hamm's Bear reclines on a 12-pack on the wall of a tavern in Bemidji, Minnesota. This vacuum-formed sign is a typical point-of-sale item that was produced after the Dancer Fitzgerald Sample advertising agency brought the bear back in 1972. The previous agency, J. Walter Thompson, had sent the bear into exile around 1969. BILL YENNE

believed to have been the first to suggest a menagerie of small animals to inhabit the mythical "Land of Sky Blue Waters." The Los Angeles animation firm of Swift-Chaplin did most of the film animation featuring the bear, and because Howard Swift created animals for Disney animated features in the 1940s, it is suggested that he may have created the bear. However, the bear was most probably created by Cleo Hovel, an illustrator and creative director at Campbell-Mithun, who ultimately did many of the drawings used in print advertising.

In the early 1950s, the new medium was television. Naturally, advertising agencies swiftly embraced it and the television commercial was born. The notion of using animated characters in television advertising was soon adopted. The

Piel Brothers Brewing Company in New York City was among the first to use it for pitching beer. They had crafted two lovable characters, Bert and Harry, whose voices were supplied by the comedy team of Bob Elliot and Ray Goulding. As popular as Bert and Harry were, nobody held a candle to the Hamm's Bear.

The Hamm's Bear made his television debut in 1953 and evolved into one of the most recognized imaginary animals in advertising history. Joined by a fox, beaver, squirrels, and other creatures, he starred in countless commercials and engaged in some outdoor activity against the backdrop of the drumming "from the Land of Sky Blue Waters" jingle orchestrated by Ernie Gavin of the WCCO radio station.

The Hamm's Bear was also adapted for print advertising and point-of-purchase items. During the 1950s and 1960s, he won numerous advertising awards for Campbell-Mithun and helped push sales of Hamm's Beer. Popular point-of-purchase items used by Hamm's during this period were the full-color, lighted motion signs. Manufactured for use in bars, they had a moving scroll with images of campfires, waterfalls, and canoes on the shore of a lake, set against a northwoods backdrop. Today these signs fetch hundreds of dollars on the collectibles market.

The brilliant advertising helped fulfill Figge's dream of expanding Hamm's into a major brand on the national scene. In 1951, Hamm's was ranked 15th nationally with a

1.2-million barrel annual output. Within three years, it was in eighth place with 2.3 million barrels. Distribution spread beyond Minnesota to encompass 30 states, plus Alaska, which was still a territory at that time.

In order to keep up with demand, Figge acquired other breweries outside of Minnesota and turned them into Hamm's breweries. In 1953, he bought the former Rainier Brewing Company facility near Seal's Stadium in San Francisco. Five years later, he bought the former Acme Brewery on 49th Street in Los Angeles that had been owned by New York's Liebmann Breweries since 1954. In 1959, he bought the Gunther Brewing Company in Baltimore. This experience was not so good, however. Resentment over the demise of Gunther as a brand, combined with bad publicity over a batch of beer that froze, made the Baltimore venture a failure. After an attempt was made to revive the Gunther brand, the brewery was sold to the Schaeffer Brewing Company of New York City in 1963. That same year, however, Hamm's bought the Gulf Brewing Company, which had operated in Houston, Texas, since 1933.

Hamm's output reached 3.8 million barrels by 1964, and it hit its peak at 4.3 million four years later. In 1965, as the Hamm Brewing Company celebrated its centennial, the company was put up for sale. Both Molson of Canada and Rheingold of New York City expressed interest in buying it, but their acquisitions were barred by the U.S. Justice Department on antitrust grounds. Hamm's was considered too big to be acquired by a brewing company. The winning bid of $10.4 million came from Heublein, a hard-liquor holding company. It was approved, and William C. Figge retired in 1966 at the age of 61.

The late 1960s and early 1970s were the days of the great brewery consolidations, and brewing companies moved to shed breweries as fast as they had been acquired in the 1950s. For Heublein-owned Hamm's, the first property to be divested was the former Gulf Brewing site in Houston, which was closed in 1967 after four years of operation. The Los Angeles brewery was closed in 1972. The giant San Francisco brewery was used

Here is a pair of Hamm's beer steins on a rough hewn table at Oktoberfest in Munich, Germany, in 1973. This stein was one of the most prized items of Hamm's memorabilia and was created as a special promotion for that year only. It was intended to publicize the brand in the context of Germany's greatest celebration of beer and beer drinking. *BILL YENNE*

between 1969 and 1973 to brew the Burgermeister ("Burgie") product.

By now, as sales began to slip, Heublein was anxious to divest the entire company. In 1973, a group of seven Hamm's distributors organized under the name Brewers Unlimited to save the Hamm's name. They operated the San Francisco brewery until 1975, when it was closed permanently.

In 1975, the Olympia Brewing Company of Tumwater, Washington, paid $14.7 million for Hamm's. Eight years later, Olympia was acquired by the Pabst Brewing Company of Milwaukee. The St. Paul brewery, where Hamm's had been brewed for 118 years,

was traded by Pabst to the Stroh Brewing Company of Detroit for a brewery in Tampa, Florida, that Stroh had picked up a year earlier when it bought Schlitz.

Production of Hamm's moved to Milwaukee, and the beer consumed in the "Land of Sky Blue Waters" was now brewed out of state. By 1985, when Paul Kalmanovitz added Pabst to the portfolio of brands held by S&P Holdings, Hamm's had lost all direct connection to the "Land of Sky Blue Waters."

As for the Hamm's Bear, his golden age ended in 1969, when Heublein dropped Campbell-Mithun as its agency in favor of New York City–based J. Walter Thompson. The new agency stressed heritage, rather than humor, and they lasted only until 1972. The Dancer Fitzgerald Sample agency came aboard and brought back the Hamm's Bear. He was briefly retired after the 1975 Olympia purchase, but rein-

In 1983, the S&P-owned Pabst Brewing Company acquired the Hamm's brand. The label didn't change much after the Pabst acquisition, but the blue became a bit brighter. Of course, the beer was no longer brewed in the Land of Sky Blue Waters. *AUTHOR COLLECTION*

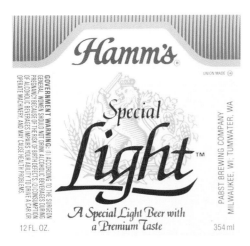

By the time Pabst acquired the Hamm's brand in 1983, the market demanded that all mass market brands be accompanied by a light version. The Hamm's Special Light label made no mention of the Land of Sky Blue Waters. *AUTHOR COLLECTION*

stated amid a great deal of "The Bear is Back" fanfare in 1978. To the surprise of virtually no one, sales went up whenever the bear returned. The Hamm's Bear continued to be used through the 1983 Pabst acquisition, but when S&P came in, advertising, for the most part, went out.

The Hamm's Bear's public career ended when neo-temperance agitators complained about cartoons being used to sell alcoholic beverages. He became one of the leading icons of brewery advertising lore and remains one of the most sought-after artifacts of breweriana.

Gleaming chrome and brilliant Lucite await the publican's steady hand. Soon the luminous amber beverage will swirl into a schooner and light the way to happiness for another patient patron. *BILL YENNE*

The classic Lone Star label from the 1940s was a veritable postcard of Texas landmarks from the San Jacinto Monument to the Alamo. Sketches of heroes from Texas and San Antonio history were also pictured and included Stephen Austin, William Barret Travis, Davy Crockett, and Sam Houston, the first president of the Republic of Texas. AUTHOR COLLECTION

CHAPTER 5

Lone Star

WHEN SURVEYING THE great beers of American history that have had a monumental regional impact, it is impossible to ignore the beer that was proudly identified as the "National Beer" of the geographically largest state in the lower 48. Texas is larger than any nation in Europe and had been an independent country for the decade leading up to its statehood in 1845. As such, Texans still perceive the Lone Star State as a nation.

Texas was owned by Spain until 1831 and then by Mexico until it achieved its independence. The area was populated by people with a Hispanic background and settlers from the United States and Europe. By the time of its statehood, there was a growing German community in and around San Antonio. With the Germans came a fondness for beer. Wilhelm (later changed to William) Menger became the first commercial lager brewer in the Lone Star State when he started the Western Brewery on Blum Street in San Antonio in 1855.

By the 1870s, San Antonio emerged as the brewing capital of the former Confederacy. In 1874 alone, William Esser, Joseph Hutzler, and C. A. Schmidt all opened commercial breweries. Two of the most historically important were J. B. Behloradsky's, which was located on the north side of San Antonio and began in 1881, and the Lone Star Brewery, which was started by Adolphus Busch on the south side in 1884.

Behloradsky's brewery, known as San Antonio Brewing after 1883, started using the Pearl Beer brand name in 1886 and officially became Pearl Brewing in 1952.

Busch is best remembered as the man who took over his father-in-law's St. Louis brewery and built Anheuser-Busch into one of America's first national mega-breweries. Although his company eventually operated a vast archipelago of Anheuser-Busch breweries throughout the United States, Busch deliberately held Lone Star separately.

Adolphus Busch had an uncanny aptitude for marketing. He certainly did well in this regard with Anheuser-Busch products and the beer from his Lone Star Brewing Company. As a brand name, Busch chose the most recognizable patriotic symbol in Texas, the Alamo. The Alamo brand was also used by William Esser's brewery between 1884 and 1895.

Adolphus Busch died in 1913, but the Lone Star Brewery operated for another five years and closed in 1918, when the shadow of Prohibition fell across the nation.

The Pearl Brewing Company was the only brewing company in San Antonio that remained in business during Prohibition. When that national nightmare finally ended in 1933, Pearl Brewing was the only brewery in the city to promptly resume brewing beer. There was an attempt to reopen the Lone Star brewery under the name Mission Brewing Company in 1933, but this venture failed. The following year, it reopened as the Sabinas Brewing Company. In 1939, it became the Champion Brewing Company, but a year later the brewery was acquired by the George Muelebach Brewing Company of Kansas City, Missouri. Muelebach Brewing had links to the Griesedieck Western Brewery of Belleville,

Alamo was the brand at the Lone Star Brewing Company when this ad appeared in the San Antonio Express in 1914. Enjoyment, pleasure, and honesty were touted. It's interesting to see an advertisement from a century ago waxing nostalgic for old-time honesty. The slug at the bottom pays lip service to the growing cloud of Prohibition and assures that Lone Star did not solicit orders from counties where a majority of voters had decided to go dry. AUTHOR COLLECTION

Illinois, which brewed the Stag brand. This brand aside, Muelebach Brewing readopted the pre-Prohibition appellation for the San Antonio facility and Lone Star was reborn.

Although the Muelebach interests divested themselves of the brewery in 1949, the Lone Star name remained and the brewery evolved as an important fixture in San Antonio and Texas. In 1954, a distribution arrangement with Screeder Distributing took Lone Star statewide. Newspaper ads proudly announced that "The beer I go for is goin' places. . . . Clear across Texas!"

Major advertising campaigns in national magazines in the 1950s and 1960s identified "The beer I go for" as "one of the world's great premium beers." Lone Star had evolved from a Texas beer to a world-class beer. The company crossed state lines in 1960 and purchased the Progress Brewing Company in Oklahoma City. This facility operated as a Lone Star Brewing Company site until 1971.

The 1970s marked a golden age for Lone Star. In this time frame it officially emerged as the National Beer of Texas. Perhaps Lone Star can more appropriately be characterized as the official beer of the outlaw movement in country music.

The outlaw movement was essentially a reaction to mainstream country music, which had, by the late 1960s, become smooth and schmaltzy. Most of the music originating from Nashville at that time had more in common with mainstream pop music than with the genre pioneered by the

The term landmark *was not applied lightly when it referred to the Buckhorn Hall of Horns. It began as the Buckhorn Saloon in downtown San Antonio in 1882. The Buckhorn was famous for displaying horns and antlers collected by Albert Friedreich on hunting trips throughout Texas. It was moved to the grounds of the Lone Star plant early in the twentieth century and served as the brewery's hospitality room. Complimentary samples of Lone Star Beer were served, but the real attraction was the fabulous collection of antlers, mounted wildlife, and antique firearms. In 1998, after the Lone Star Brewery closed, the collection was reacquired by Friedreich's descendents and moved to a new Buckhorn Saloon away from the Lone Star campus.* AUTHOR COLLECTION

likes of Hank Williams and Ernest Tubb a generation before. The outlaw movement sought to create a genre that relied more on rockabilly-style lead guitar than lush string sections. It was more of the type of music that one would expect in a honky-tonk bar, and it was performed by people wearing jeans and cowboy boots rather than suits and ties.

More important in terms of how Lone Star Beer fit into the mix, the outlaw artists relocated themselves

In the 1960s, Lone Star competed with the national brands by de-emphasizing anything unique about its heritage or character. Lone Star started brewing in Oklahoma City in 1960, but in 1966, Schlitz entered Lone Star's back yard with a big new facility in Longview, Texas. AUTHOR COLLECTION

In 1959, Lone Star emphasized it German roots in its advertising and pictured its Heidelberg Beer Garden in San Antonio. The city was settled in the mid-nineteenth century by a sizable number of German immigrants, a fact that helped San Antonio become the brewing capital of Texas. Within a generation, the emphasis changed entirely and Lone Star's image shifted from burgermeisters to cowboys. AUTHOR COLLECTION

You deserve the best ....*nothing less !*

When you spend your money for a fine beer, you expect the best and have a right to get it. The beer in this glass came from a brew that cost $9,300 to make. A million dollars couldn't have brewed you a finer beer. That's why the dollar and change you spend for a Lone Star 6-pack is the world's best buy.

one of the world's great premium beers

Visit the Lone Star Pavilion at HemisFair'68

LONE STAR BREWING COMPANY / SAN ANTONIO / OKLAHOMA CITY

In 1968, San Antonio celebrated its World's Fair, which was known as the HemisFair because it highlighted the Western Hemisphere. As a hometown brewer, Lone Star opened its own pavilion. This ad for a six-pack of Lone Star stubbies, with its strangely convoluted text, invited folks to visit the brewery's pavilion.
AUTHOR COLLECTION

from Nashville to Austin, Texas. The leading exponents of the movement had roots in Texas. These included singers and songwriters such as Willie Nelson, Waylon Jennings, Jerry Jeff Walker, Billy Joe Shaver, and David Allen Coe. The fact that Nelson had previously been a very successful Nashville songwriter underscored the idea that the outlaw movement was a true rebellion.

The popularity of the outlaws became legendary. In 1976, Nelson and Jennings, along with Tompall Glaser and Jennings' wife, Jessi Colter, released an album entitled *Wanted: The Outlaws* that became the first country music album to sell a million units and go platinum.

This is the Lone Star Brewery on the south side of San Antonio as it appeared during most of the latter half of the twentieth century. It was a major industrial center and important San Antonio employer, but it was also the spiritual center of Texas beer-drinking during this era. BILL YENNE

Lone Star Beer played a prominent role in the movement by sponsoring concerts and positioning its advertising in conjunction with anything related to the outlaw music and the personality cults of the Texas-based outlaws. Willie Nelson's annual Fourth of July picnics, which were actually enormous outdoor concerts, were sponsored by the "National Beer of Texas."

Lone Star even found its way into the lyrics of country songs. Red Steagall's 1976 song, "Lone Star Beer and Bob Wills Music," recorded by David Allan Coe, featured the line "Tell all the ladies I'm single, tell Lone Star Beer that I'm dry."

One of the significant anthems of the outlaw movement was the song "Mamas, Don't Let Your Babies Grow Up to be Cowboys," written by Ed and Patsy Bruce and immortalized

Somewhat the worse for wear, this classic Lone Star can from the 1970s rests on a fence post somewhere in west Texas and invites a cowboy to have a little target practice. BILL YENNE

by Willie Nelson. It paid tribute to a pair of San Antonio–made commercial products that were essential elements of the Texas/outlaw ethos with the line "Lone Star belt buckles and old faded Levi's, and each night begins a new day."

Ironically, just as Lone Star was beginning its new day as the National Beer of Texas, it ceased to be Texas-owned. Beginning in 1976, it was sold, resold, and owned by a succession of out-of-state companies, including Washington's Olympia, Wisconsin's Heileman, Michigan's Stroh, and Pabst.

The sale to Olympia Brewing Company occurred in 1976, and in 1983, when Olympia was acquired by Pabst, Lone Star was sold to

Turn left on West Jones Avenue for Lone Star. This is the entrance to the Lone Star facility on the south side of San Antonio late on a January afternoon. The Buckhorn Hall of Horns was still located there at the time this photo was taken, but today the beer and the horns are gone. BILL YENNE

An empty Lone Star glass sits on a kitchen table in Luckenbach, Texas, on the morning after. Such a phrase might have been the subject of a 1977 outlaw country song. In fact, Waylon Jennings did put Luckenbach on the map that year, and Lone Star was more than likely involved in the process. BILL YENNE

G. Heileman of LaCrosse, Wisconsin. During the 1980s, Heileman became famous for its collection of beers with strong regional identification. In addition to Lone Star and Olympia, these included Seattle's Rainier, Portland's Weinhard, Grain Belt of Minneapolis, and the former Griesedieck label, Stag.

In the late 1990s, Lone Star was swept up in what some brewing industry alarmists referred to as the industry's "final consolidation." Heileman went bankrupt in 1991 and was out of business in 1996. Its brand names were sold to the Stroh Brewing Company of Detroit. However, in 1999, John Stroh III announced that the Stroh family would pull the plug on the family business a year short of its

150th birthday. The Stroh family sold its Stroh and Heileman brands to Miller and Pabst.

Pabst, which had owned the San Antonio–based Pearl Brewing since 1988, acquired the Lone Star brand, but promptly closed the brewery on the site where beer had been brewed for 115 years. Production was moved to the Pearl plant on the north side of town. Between June 1999 and December 2002, both Pearl and Lone Star were produced at the same facility. A further chapter in the saga came at the end of 2002, when Pabst, the one-time largest brewer in America, ceased to brew beer entirely.

This poster, photographed in 1994 on the side of an old barn around Nacodoches, celebrates Lone Star's sponsorship of Texas rodeos. Although the brand had not been Texas-owned for nearly two decades, it still maintained a link to its roots in the Lone Star State. BILL YENNE

This 1983 Lone Star label still proclaims the brand as the National Beer of Texas, although when it was issued, Lone Star was part of the portfolio of regional brands owned by Wisconsin's Heileman. Lone Star had been owned by out-of-state interests since 1976. AUTHOR COLLECTION

From the beginning of 2003, Pabst became a "virtual brewer." The former Pearl Brewery on the north side of San Antonio was sold and all of the Pabst brands were contract-brewed by other companies. A majority of the Pabst-owned brands were brewed under license by the Miller Brewing Company. Pearl and Lone Star were produced in Texas at Miller's facility in Fort Worth.

Meanwhile, Levi Strauss and Company—which produced the denim jeans favored by cowboys at several factories in the San Antonio area—also left town. By the time Pearl and Lone Star ceased to be brewed in San Antonio, Levi's ceased to be made anywhere in the United States.

This attractive 1996 point-of-sale piece makes reference to the underground Texas urban legend about giant armadillos attacking Lone Star Beer trucks. AUTHOR COLLECTION

Country singer Tracie Lynn is pictured here with an old Lone Star sign. Tracie grew up in Portland, Texas, and spent several years writing songs in Nashville. She is now based in Austin. Well-known for her songs, such as "I Know You're Lying Because Your Lips Are Moving," she is popular throughout the Lone Star State. She recently signed a sponsorship deal with Lone Star and has recorded radio advertising. "It has been my favorite beer for years," she said. "How cool [is it] to be sponsored by the National Beer of Texas." MELISSA WEBB, COURTESY OF TRACIE LYNN

The Lucky Lager "Flying L" logo was introduced in the late 1970s before the San Francisco brewery was closed in 1978. It was used long after the brand faded from prominence and became a minor product within the Pabst portfolio. AUTHOR COLLECTION

CHAPTER 6

Lucky Lager

W HILE MANY OF THE great breweries in American brewing history trace their heritage back into the nineteenth century, the General Brewing Corporation is an example of a brewing company that did not exist before Prohibition but became a major player in the years following that national debacle.

In the years following the repeal of Prohibition, trucks were the standard means of delivering beer within a city, but draft-horse teams still evoked fond memories and were used for special events. General Brewing Company began operations here on Newhall Street in San Francisco in 1934 using the legendary Lucky Lager brand name. AUTHOR COLLECTION

General began operations at 2601 Newhall Street in San Francisco in 1934, the year following the repeal.

The crusty corporate name was not right as a brand name, so they searched for the correct appellation for General's flagship lager. A brainstorming session conjured up a cluster of suggestions that are all lost to time. The one that won out became a legend in America's Far West. A love of alliteration led to the adoption of the name "Lucky Lager."

Although the corporate name remained General Brewing for a time, the beer was universally known as

Lucky. With this in mind, the company later renamed itself Lucky Lager Brewing twice. Over the coming decades, the corporate name reverted back to General twice, and there were years when the two existed as separate, but associated and interrelated, entities.

Soon after the first kegs of Lucky rolled out the door, the Newhall plant became one of San Francisco's major brewing centers, rivaled only by the Acme facility across town. The plant was able to accommodate the demand for Lucky Lager through the waning years of the Depression and into World War II. However, after World War II, California's population exploded as its economy boomed. The thirsty workers needed more beer, and California's home-grown brewing companies were anxious to oblige.

Lucky Lager quickly became an important cultural fixture and promoted itself in everything from billboards near Seals Stadium, San Francisco's Pacific Coast League baseball park, to popular radio programs. One of the best

"One of the world's really fine beers"

● LUCKY LAGER is truly "one of the world's really fine beers." For Lucky Lager is a product of highest quality . . . made in one of the world's most modern and sanitary breweries . . . from the choicest ingredients that money can buy . . . under the **exclusive** Lucky Lager brewing process. ● For beer at its best, insist on Lucky Lager . . . the **dated** beer.

General Brewing Corporation
SAN FRANCISCO :: LOS ANGELES

LUCKY LAGER
THE ORIGINAL AGE-DATED BEER

remembered of the latter was *Lucky Lager Dance Time*, a live music program aired on KSFO in the years after World War II.

Celebrity endorsements played a role as well. While many beers used sports figures, Lucky Lager landed Arthur Fiedler, the conductor of the Boston Pops Orchestra, who came west in 1954 to serve as the summer conductor of the San Francisco Symphony Orchestra. It turned out that Fiedler was a beer lover and a fan of prize fights. The conductor quaffed his first Lucky at a fight in San Francisco and his comments led to an advertising campaign.

"I like to watch boxers in action," said Fiedler. "Looking for champions is a hobby of mine. That's how I found Lucky Lager. It's the champion of beer. It's great to relax with a cold bottle of Lucky Lager. Every glass tastes just as smooth as the last."

While San Francisco had been California's major metropolis for the better part of a century, it was eclipsed by Los Angeles before World War II, and the major postwar population growth in the Golden State was in southern California. In 1935, Acme was the first California brewer with major operations in San Francisco and Los Angeles, and all the major national

This 1952 ad in the Alaska Weekly newspaper had a tagline that only mentioned the Lucky Lager brewery in Vancouver, Washington. This was probably because all of the Lucky sold in Alaska was shipped up the Columbia River from this facility. AUTHOR COLLECTION

Regional lines were drawn by the time this stylish young lady paused to pose with her pilsner glass of Lucky Lager in 1950. There were eastern beers that started to make inroads in the California market, and there were western beers, such as Lucky. AUTHOR COLLECTION

brewers arrived in the early 1950s. General, renamed as Lucky Lager Brewing Company in 1948, went south in 1949.

In the late 1940s, before the arrival of the nationals, the major brew players in southern California were Acme, Grace Brothers, Maier Brewing Company, and the Los Angeles Brewing Company. Grace Brothers, which also went by the name Southern Brewing (not to be confused with Southern California Brewing), evolved from a post-Prohibition start-up, but Southern California Brewing dated back to 1897. Maier evolved from the brewery started by Edward Preuss in 1874.

As was the case with General and Lucky Lager, Southern California Brewing was best known by its brand names. During Prohibition, these were Zesto beverage products, but since 1934, the flagship brand was Eastside Beer. For the Maier Brewing Company, the brand was ABC.

When General/Lucky arrived in 1948, the company followed its rival to the east side of Los Angeles County and chose a site for a brewery in the city of Azusa. Whereas General/Lucky survived the impending invasion of the nationals, both Eastside and Acme sold out. The Eastside facility became the first Pabst brewery in California in 1953, and Acme sold its brewery to Rheingold the following year.

As the national breweries arrived in the Far West, a spontaneous cultural phenomenon quickly came into place in beer advertising. This phenomenon was the strict delineation between homegrown Western Beer and Eastern Beer, the beer made by the interloping nationals. Lucky Lager was Western Beer, and when Acme and Eastside faded away, it became *the* Western Beer within California. With this in mind, it is easy to understand the

It's party time for Lucky Lager retailers, and everyone is here for a good time. A couple of the people gathered for this October 1953 celebration are definitely in a good mood. The brand rode high in the 1950s and eclipsed Acme as the "National Beer of California," and held its own against eastern brands.
AUTHOR COLLECTION

Jack Kramer was one of America's greatest tennis players when Lucky Lager tapped him for an endorsement in 1955. The 1947 Wimbledon singles champ and U.S. champ in 1946 and 1947, he turned promoter in 1952 and later worked as a television commentator. He conceived the Grand Prix series of tournaments that led to a Masters Championship. He also enjoyed a cold glass of Lucky. AUTHOR COLLECTION

When Boston Pops conductor Arthur Fiedler spent the summer of 1954 as a guest conductor at the San Francisco Symphony Orchestra, he discovered Lucky Lager at a boxing match. He liked it so much he agreed to an endorsement deal. AUTHOR COLLECTION

brand's signature double entendre tagline: "It's Lucky When You Live in California." As Lucky Lager grew in prominence throughout the West during the 1950s and 1960s, the line was modified to read "It's Lucky When You Live in America."

During this period, Lucky Lager successfully operated a multisite regional empire that paralleled those being created in the East at the same time by the major national brands. Excluding their California and Texas operations, neither Schlitz, Pabst, nor Anheuser Busch had breweries spread over a larger area than Lucky Lager at its peak.

The first major step toward transforming Lucky from a California to a regional brand came in 1950, with the acquisition of the Interstate Brewing Company in Vancouver, Washington, directly across the Columbia River from Portland, Oregon. The Interstate, obviously named for the fact that the center of the Vancouver-Portland metro area was across a state line, was founded in 1939. Interstate was created from the Star Brewery Company, which had been in business since 1894. The company's roots went back to 1856, when it was the first commercial brewery in what is now Washington State.

Founded by John (Johann) Muench as the Vancouver Brewery, the facility was taken over in 1859 by young Henry Weinhard, who became the godfather of Oregon brewing. In

This tableau of a night at a Los Angeles tavern in the early 1950s features many of the icons of the era: a guy, three gals, access to the jukebox, and a couple of Lucky Lager longnecks. Note that there are also two elaborate beer steins on the bar. Although the young woman on the right seems to be drinking from a glass, the steins definitely were there for decoration. AUTHOR COLLECTION

Rice, beans, and a couple of beers. This young couple is having a bite to eat before heading out to the dance club. They're both drinking Lucky Lager, while the photographer has the quart size of Eastside. After Lucky Lager opened its southern California brewery in 1948, the two brands had a serious rivalry. In 1953, Eastside faded from the scene when Pabst took over its brewery. AUTHOR COLLECTION

1862, when Weinhard went on to bigger and better things down in Portland, he sold the Vancouver Brewery to Anton Young. In turn, Anton Young sold the brewery to Louis Gerlinger, who rechristened it as the Star Brewery Company in 1894. A half-century later, it was the springboard to Lucky Lager's major market penetration into the Northwest and the intermountain West, especially Washington, Oregon, and Montana.

It may have been "Lucky When You Live in" much of the Northwest and Mountain West, but at the corporate headquarters, the 1960s was a time for General. In 1963, the Newhall Street brewery in San Francisco was renamed the General Brewing Corporation, and the Azusa facility became the Southern California Division of the General Brewing Corporation. It was not until the following year that the Vancouver site was renamed the Northern Division of the General Brewing Corporation. Also in 1964, the Salt Lake City site became a branch of the Newhall Street incarnation of the General Brewing Corporation.

The 1960s marked the beginning of industry consolidation. The power of Eastern Beer heavily impacted the westerners. A generation later, a

A further step to secure Lucky Lager as the leading brand in the mountain West came in 1960 with the Fisher Brewing Company in Salt Lake City. Founded in 1884, Fisher was one of a half-dozen breweries that operated in the Utah capital in the late nineteenth century, but it was the only one to successfully resume brewing after Prohibition. The facility was brought online as a Lucky operation, and the brand dominated the northern Rockies during the 1960s. At the time, Coors was not yet available much beyond its home in Colorado.

The beer beer-drinkers drink!

12 OUNCES LUCKY LAGER

GENERAL BREWING CORP., SAN FRANCISCO, AZUSA, CALIF. – VANCOUVER, WASH. – SALT LAKE CITY, UTAH

The headline in this ad from the program of the 1965 Roller Derby International League program could not have been more to the point. By this time, Lucky Lager included its Salt Lake City brewery in its tagline and promoted its new easy-to-use pull tab. The proliferation of discarded pull tabs led to the pop-top that is still in use today. AUTHOR'S COLLECTION

NET CONTENTS 11 FL. OZ.

LUCKY BREWERIES, INC. SAN FRANCISCO, CALIF.® VANCOUVER, WASH.

Lucky Light Beer

This beer is remarkably non-filling. *A special, more costly brewing process gives our beer its unusual lightness and smoothness. This, combined with quality brewing ingredients has made Lucky Light one of Oregon's most popular light beers.*

In the late 1970s, Lucky Lager joined with all other major brewing companies and marketed a light variation. The regular lager was color-coded in red, and Lucky Light was light orange. AUTHOR COLLECTION

renaissance swept the West as craft brewers managed to outmaneuver the national brands with superior quality. In the 1960s, the regionals erroneously believed they had to compete on price. Ultimately it would be their undoing.

Beginning in the late 1960s, the once-great brand behaved like a rudderless ship. Existing breweries were sold, and new breweries were bought and sold. The name was changed and changed back. One needs a scorecard to keep track of the corporate meanderings of Lucky and General during this period.

GENERAL BREWING COMPANY • VANCOUVER, WA. 98660

SAN FRANCISCO, CA. 94124 •

Lucky BOCK BEER
The Finest of Them All

NET CONTENTS 11 FLUID OUNCES

To save money, General was forced to divest property. The Azusa site was sold to Miller Brewing in 1966, and the Salt Lake City plant was closed in 1967. Two years later, the two surviving General Brewing Corporation sites were renamed again for the brand name, but they were owned by General. In 1971, with two plants operating as Lucky Breweries Inc., General Brewing acquired two additional plants as General breweries in the same geographic regions as those that had been divested in 1966 and 1967.

The "new" General breweries were the former Maier Brewing Company in Los Angeles and the former Walter Brewing Company in Pueblo, Colorado. The latter traced its history back to the company started by Carl Roth in 1889. It was officially named the General Brewing Company of Colorado, but it did business under the Walter Brewing Company name. These two 1971 acquisitions were closed in 1974 and 1975, respectively.

Before 1950, many American brewers produced an annual bock beer, but this practice faded as mass market beer became lighter and had a more neutral flavor. This rare label recalls that Lucky Lager briefly resumed the practice in the late 1970s. AUTHOR COLLECTION

In 1972, the General Brewing name was reinstated for the final time for all of the companies and breweries. In 1975, the entire family was acquired by Paul Kalmanovitz and incorporated into his S&P Holdings along with Falstaff. In keeping with Kalmanovitz's drastic downsizing paradigm, the Los Angeles and Pueblo plants and the original brewery on Newhall Street were closed.

Between 1975 and 1985, only the big brewery in Vancouver, Washington, remained of the network of western breweries that had once brewed Lucky Lager. In 1985, Kalmanovitz closed and dismantled the entire plant and shipped it to China, where it was reassembled in Zhouging.

Lucky Lager survived as a brand name and was contract-brewed by third-party breweries. Its last hurrah was as the de facto house brand of the unrelated Lucky grocery store chain. The latter was absorbed by the Albertson's chain in 1999, and the various Lucky-branded products were discontinued.

This juxtaposition of artifacts contrasts an opener from the Golden Age of Lucky Lager with a pair of cans from the later years. These cans from the 1980s have pop-tops and don't need the vintage church key to open them. BILL YENNE

The last Lucky Lager brewery in operation was here at the corner of Columbia Street and West Seventh in Vancouver, Washington. Beer had been brewed here for nearly a century when Lucky Lager took over the site in 1950. In 1985, about a decade after this picture was taken, the brewery was completely dismantled, shipped to China, and reassembled in Zhaoging. AUTHOR COLLECTION

The Miller High Life label that was used during the 1980s included the Miller Eagle logo that dates back to the nineteenth century and continues to be prominent on Miller Genuine Draft packaging. The neck label from the 1980s featured type only.
COURTESY JEFF WAALKES, MILLER BREWING COMPANY

CHAPTER 7

Miller High Life

MANY OF THE GREAT

old brands and trademarks that are

profiled in this book are icons of a

bygone era. They came and went

with the fortunes of once-proud

independent brewing companies

that have faded from national

prominence. Miller's Girl in the

Moon, on the other hand, hitched

her fortune to the rising star.

The brewing company that evolved into Miller Brewing originated with the Plank Road Brewery, founded by Charles Best in 1850 in Wauwatosa, Wisconsin. *COURTESY OF JEFF WAALKES, MILLER BREWING COMPANY*

The Miller Brewing Company began the twentieth century as one of a group of important brewing companies in Milwaukee, but while its neighbors faded, Miller ended the century as the second-largest brewing company in the United States for more than two decades.

Miller Brewing evolved from the Menominee Valley Brewery, which was established in 1850 in Wauwatosa, Wisconsin. Charles Best, the founder, was the son of Jacob Best, who had started the

Born in Germany in 1824, Frederick Miller learned the brewing trade in France and started brewing in Milwaukee in 1855. He died in 1888, more than a decade before his family adopted the Girl in the Moon as a trademark and High Life as a brand.
BILL YENNE

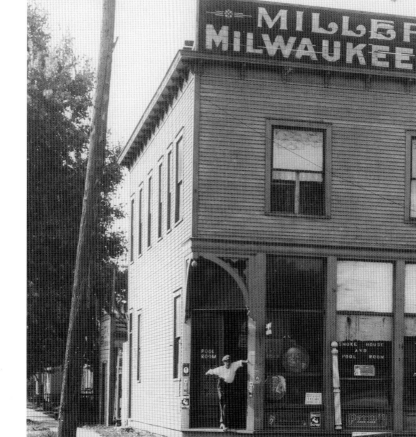

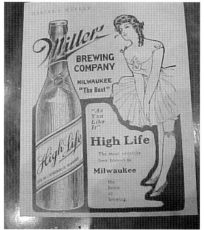

This ad from Harper's Weekly in early 1903 shows a Miller Girl associated with the product, although she was not the Miller Girl. The moon was added four years later. COURTESY OF TICE NICHOLS, MILLER BREWING COMPANY

In the late nineteenth century, all of the major American brewing companies operated tied houses, company-owned taverns that specialized in the product of the parent company. COURTESY OF TICE NICHOLS, MILLER BREWING COMPANY

In the initial stages of the evolution of the Miller brand, the word Milwaukee was the key word. This image of an early Miller Brewing distribution depot shows the Miller eagle logo that is still used today. COURTESY OF TICE NICHOLS, MILLER BREWING COMPANY

Empire Brewery in Milwaukee six years earlier. Charles' new brewery was best known as the Plank Road Brewery because the streets in timber-rich Wisconsin were paved with wood.

Although the Best family was a fixture on the Milwaukee brewing scene for many years in the middle of the nineteenth century, Charles' tenure was short-lived. By 1853, he had closed up shop. In 1854, the brewery reopened under a young German immigrant whose Anglicized name was Frederick Edward John Miller. The brewery's name changed to Miller Brewing, although the company briefly revived the Plank Road Brewery name for specialty products in the mid-1980s and 1990s.

A powerful team of draft horses prepares for the morning delivery and heads out from the Miller Brewing Company branch depot on the south side of Chicago. COURTESY OF TICE NICHOLS, MILLER BREWING COMPANY

This vintage photograph dates from the first decade of the twentieth century, shortly after the High Life brand was introduced in 1903. In the image, a satisfied customer steps from Mathkirar's Tavern. COURTESY OF TICE NICHOLS, MILLER BREWING COMPANY

This detail from the 1907 Girl in the Moon tray shows the credit line and copyright notice of Albert C. Paul, the Miller Brewing Company employee who first introduced the Girl in the Moon into Miller advertising. COURTESY OF TICE NICHOLS, MILLER BREWING COMPANY

This Miller Brewing Company lighted sign dates from the 1930s and is typical of the electric point-of-sale pieces that brewing companies in the United States introduced after Prohibition. COURTESY OF TICE NICHOLS, MILLER BREWING COMPANY

Frederick Miller was born in 1824 into an influential family from Riedlingen in the southern German state of Wurtemburg. He moved to France when he was 14 and became an apprentice at his uncle's brewery in the Lorraine city of Nancy. He later recrossed the Rhine to take over operations at the Royal Hohenzollern brewery in Sigmaringen. In 1854, Miller and his wife, Josephine, came to the United States with a sizable nest egg.

After living briefly in New York City, the Millers and their young son, Joseph, relocated to Milwaukee, where Frederick acquired the Plank Road Brewery. Company records indicate that he brewed his first batch of beer in 1855, and he opened a beer hall on East Water Street in Milwaukee in 1857.

Frederick Miller and his wife did not have an easy life in Wisconsin. They lost several children in infancy, and in April 1860, Josephine died, possibly in childbirth, or perhaps from cholera, which claimed more than 60 people a week in the area in 1860. To complicate matters, the Civil War began in 1861 and negatively impacted Miller's business.

Frederick Miller married Lisette Gross in 1860, and they had several children. Frederick died in 1888 and was succeeded by two of his sons. Ernest was active in company affairs until 1922, and Frederick A. Miller was involved until 1947. Miller's company remained under family ownership until a controlling share was sold to the W. R. Grace Company in 1966. Four years later, control passed to Philip Morris.

In 2002, after 33 years in the portfolio of a tobacco company, Miller was sold to London-based South African Breweries. The transaction created the world's

This charger from 1907 shows the Miller Girl in the year she was first pictured on the moon. The costume and the hat remained essentially unchanged. Typically, a tray with an identical design served as a companion piece to the wall-mounted charger. COURTESY OF TICE NICHOLS, MILLER BREWING COMPANY

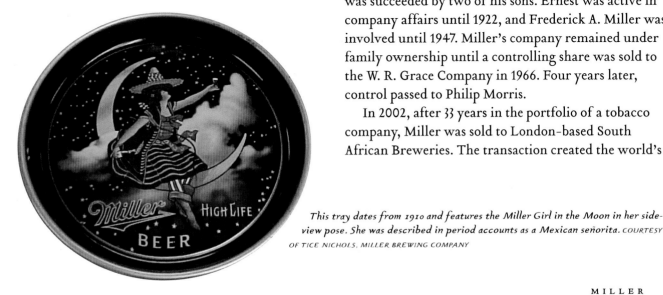

This tray dates from 1910 and features the Miller Girl in the Moon in her side-view pose. She was described in period accounts as a Mexican señorita. COURTESY OF TICE NICHOLS, MILLER BREWING COMPANY

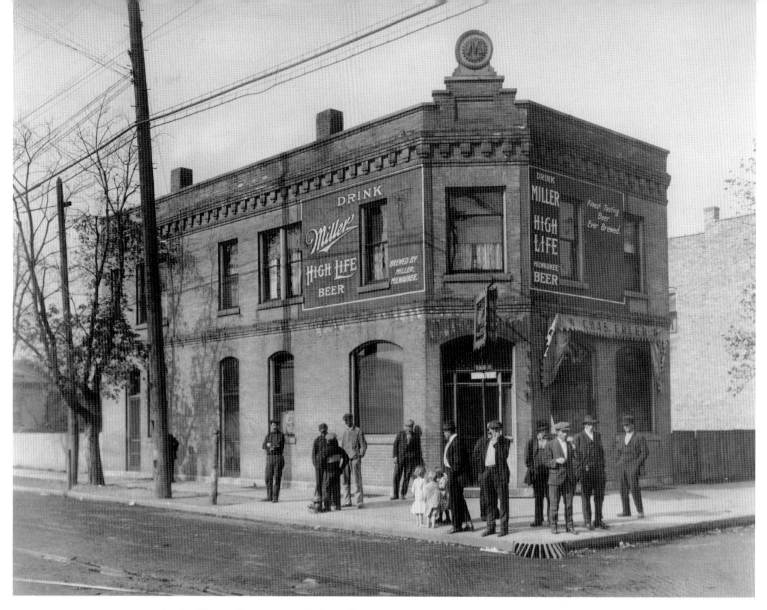

It was a family affair on the street outside this Miller-tied house in Kenosha, Wisconsin. The Miller High Life name was well established in the signage at this establishment managed by Charles Erler. *COURTESY OF TICE NICHOLS, MILLER BREWING COMPANY*

The unique attire of the Girl in the Moon was not solely for use in advertising pieces. This scene from a 1937 mask ball shows a whole bevy of Miller High Life Girls in costume. *COURTESY OF TICE NICHOLS, MILLER BREWING COMPANY*

"MILLER HIGH LIFE GIRLS" OF 1937 MASK BALL

A PURE TONIC BEVERAGE
DOES NOT CONTAIN ½ OF 1% OF ALCOHOL BY VOLUME
NTS 12 FLUID OZ   SERVE COLD

High Life

PERMIT Nº W·L·101
MADE AND BOTTLED BY
MILLER HIGH LIFE CO.
MILWAUKEE. WIS.

Miller
HIGH LIFE
BREW
MILWAUKEE

During Prohibition,
the Miller Brewing
Company retained
the Girl in the Moon
and the Miller High
Life brand, but
during the 1920s, the
product was brew
rather than beer.
Any reference to
"the Champagne of
Bottled Beer" was
placed on ice until
1933. COURTESY OF
TICE NICHOLS, MILLER
BREWING COMPANY

second-largest brewing company behind Anheuser-Busch. The name of this new entity is SABMiller.

Through the years, Miller had a variety of brand names. In 1975, the company led the industry in the creation of reduced-calorie or light beer. Consultants pointed out that beer drinkers were more likely to be men, so in an effort to attract more women, major brewers introduced a new, lower-calorie beer. Miller's entry, known as Lite or Miller Lite, was the first reduced calorie beer and became the world's leading light beer, outselling Anheuser Busch's Michelob Light and Bud Light. Overall, the light beer phenomenon pioneered by Miller Lite helped fuel a 7.5 percent increase in overall beer consumption, the largest increase in the United States since World War II. By the mid-1980s, light beers had secured a permanent niche in the North American market and accounted for 22 percent of all beer sold.

The backbone of the Miller product line through most of the century was the brewery's longtime flagship brand, Miller High Life. Rolled out amid great fanfare on December 30, 1903, Miller High Life was named by Frederick's son, Ernest. The idea was to position the beer as a stylish product for the most elite consumers. To underscore this, the Miller High Life slogan, "the Champagne of Bottled Beer," was coined in 1906.

The new brand was identified with a young lady, who appeared in Miller High Life advertising during 1904. Through the years there have been

For most of her career, the Girl in the Moon has served solely as the representative of Miller High Life. In 1938, however, she was called upon to serve on the distinctive red label of the short-lived Miller Select Beer. COURTESY OF TICE NICHOLS, MILLER BREWING COMPANY

This extremely rare Miller Girl in the Moon point-of-sale piece was produced in the early 1940s and designed to fit on top of a cash register or on a back bar. COURTESY OF TICE NICHOLS, MILLER BREWING COMPANY

many stories about the mysterious woman who became one of the most recognized trademarks in American brewing history. It was rumored she was the daughter of someone important, and from time to time, a woman has come forward to assert that she was the mystery girl. Any of these rumors and claims would have made for a good story had any of them been true. In fact, she was not based on any specific person.

She was "discovered" in 1902 by Albert C. Paul, who was then the advertising and marketing manager at Miller Brewing. Described in period accounts as "a Mexican señorita," she was carved into a 10-inch piece of wood from an old wooden box. Holding a short whip, she was dressed in the gear that one might expect of an equestrian performer in a circus.

Although Paul acquired the embossed piece in 1902, he didn't have the notion to associate the girl from the box with Miller High Life when it rolled out in 1903. Several other girls had been pictured in Miller advertising, and other girls were used in early 1904 to pitch Miller High Life before Paul had his brainstorm. When he did, the girl in the equestrian costume became the Miller Girl.

Today she is known universally as the "Girl in the Moon," but Paul did not actually place her on the moon until 1907. Originally, as in the prototype acquired by Paul in 1902, the image of the Miller Girl was a side view. Between 1904 and 1907, she stood on a beer crate.

Although the Girl in the Moon was officially associated with Miller High Life, she helped Miller pitch other brands. When Prohibition was imposed on the United States, she remained, but Miller High Life went away and she became the spokesmodel for Miller Brew. Her depiction remained largely unchanged during this period, but she was relieved of her whip. When Prohibition ended in 1933,

In this attractive holiday season ad from 1948, the Miller Girl in the Moon turned to face her audience. Until that year, the Girl in the Moon had always appeared in profile. Since 1948, she has been used both ways, with the side view used whenever a retro look was desired. AUTHOR COLLECTION

These lighted cash register tops, made of chrome, were introduced in 1953 and were high-end point-of-sale pieces.
COURTESY OF TICE NICHOLS, MILLER BREWING COMPANY

Miller High Life returned, advertised once again by the young Girl in the Moon.

Miller Select beer was a short-lived product association for the Girl in the Moon. She appeared on the red label of this beer, which was introduced in 1938. This brand was the first beer that the Miller Brewing Company ever placed in cans.

Ten years later, Miller decided that the Girl in the Moon should make eye contact with her viewers, and four decades of her being pictured in a side view came to an end. For the next two decades, the Girl in the Moon remained largely unchanged, although by the 1960s, she figured less and less in Miller advertising. In 1968, two years after the family sold controlling interest in the company to W. R. Grace, the Girl in the Moon was deleted from the Miller High Life label.

This fragile celluloid dangler pin appeared in 1955. The circular part at the top shows the classic Girl in the Moon side-view image. At the bottom, the iconography comes full circle. We see her face as it appeared after 1948, but she's standing on a box as she had when she was first introduced in 1903. COURTESY OF TICE NICHOLS, MILLER BREWING COMPANY

In 1986, a decade after the introduction of Miller Lite, the company added a new product known as Miller Genuine Draft or MGD. It was a cold-filtered beer that was not heat-pasteurized; therefore it was like a draft beer. Over the next decade, the new product gradually became more prominent than the Champagne of Bottled Beer.

As Miller High Life receded from prominence compared to its younger siblings, it seemed that the Girl in the Moon would be forgotten. This changed in 1997 when Miller Brewing decided to undertake a new packaging and marketing campaign to reacquaint beer drinkers with Miller High Life. With this, the Girl in the Moon reappeared on Miller High Life packaging after a hiatus of nearly three decades. The new campaign was also characterized by a new variation on the classic slogan. The Champagne of Bottled Beer was now the Champagne of Beer.

"Miller High Life's revitalization focuses on traditional values of simplicity, hard work, and common sense; values shared by its drinkers," said Bruce Winterton, the High Life category brand director. "Miller High Life's timeless brand and its recharged packaging, advertising, and promotions will further strengthen its appeal to Miller High Life loyalists, while attracting a new generation of beer drinkers."

In 2004, the Miller Girl celebrated her centennial back where she belonged and promoted Miller High Life from her lofty vantage point upon the moon.

This wall-mounted charger with the Miller Girl in the Moon facing forward was introduced some time after 1948 and was used as a point-of-sale piece in taverns and other retail venues.
COURTESY OF TICE NICHOLS, MILLER BREWING COMPANY

This collection of vintage Girl in the Moon point-of-sale pieces is on display on the executive floor at the Miller Brewing Company headquarters in Milwaukee. The post-1948 statue on the right features the Girl in the Moon in full view. *COURTESY OF TICE NICHOLS, MILLER BREWING COMPANY*

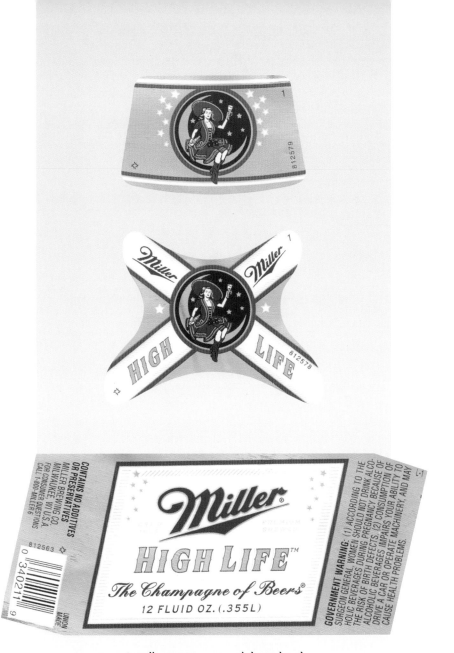

In 1998, Miller Brewing restored the Girl in the Moon to the neck label and the "soft cross" on Miller High Life bottles. The main label was also redesigned and restored the reference to "the Champagne of Beers." Although the girl did not appear on the main label, stars were used to tie it to the image of her at the top of the bottle. *COURTESY OF TICE NICHOLS AND DAVE HERREWIG, MILLER BREWING COMPANY*

Photographed at the Miller Brewing Company hospitality room in Milwaukee, this retro Girl in the Moon mirror was released as a point-of-sale piece in the 1970s. *COURTESY OF TICE NICHOLS, MILLER BREWING COMPANY*

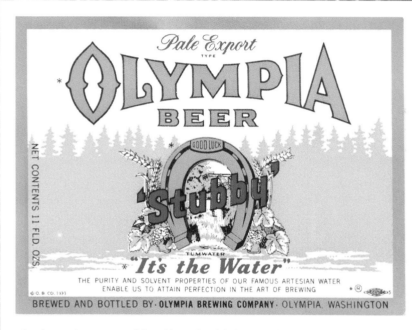

The classic Olympia waterfall and horseshoe label remained essentially unchanged for several decades after World War II. The 11-ounce stubby was the brand's signature package during its golden age. *AUTHOR COLLECTION*

CHAPTER 8

Olympia

THE LEGENDARY slogan said, "It's the water!" and that said it all. No beer in America was so closely associated with a particular water source, and no water source in America ever played such an important role in the history of a great brewery from the beginning to the bitter end.

The stories of the great German-American brewmasters all begin with learning their trade in the old country. This wasn't the case with Leopold Friederich Schmidt. He left his home in the Oberhessen town of Dornassenheim to go to sea on the North Atlantic. By the time he made the decision to stay in the United States permanently, he was already the veteran of a number of transatlantic crossings. The year was 1866 and Leopold Schmidt was 20 years old.

Schmidt worked on the Great Lakes for a time, and then on the Mississippi and Missouri rivers. As with many young men of his era, he was bitten by the gold bug and traveled into the West in search of opportunities in the mines. In 1875, he

reached Butte, Montana. Butte was known as the richest hill on earth and was Montana Territory's largest city and a major mineral-producing site.

Leopold Schmidt came to Butte in search of one kind of gold, but found another—lager. In 1876, America's centennial year, Schmidt founded the Centennial Brewery. Schmidt's operation was Butte's first major commercial brewery and a major success story.

Two years later, he traveled back to Germany and made his first Atlantic round trip as a passenger. While at home, Schmidt completed a course of study at a German brewmasters' school and got married. He returned to Butte in 1879 to resume his role at the brewery. Leopold and Johanna's first son, Peter, was born in 1880.

The lady seems right at home on the plate ledge of a Victorian tavern near Port Angeles, Washington. This tray is a twentieth-century reproduction, but the illustration was used in Olympia advertising materials in the nineteenth century. BILL YENNE

Before Leopold Schmidt discovered the artesian water in the hills above Olympia, he was the premier brewery owner in Butte, Montana, for two decades. Butte's miners had a reputation for being thirsty, and Schmidt addressed their needs. BILL YENNE

OLYMPIA BREWING COMPANY

This aerial view shows the full extent of the Olympia Brewery campus in its halcyon days. The brewery itself is in the center, just above the Capitol Boulevard bridge. The loading dock is in the lower right. The gold dome of the Washington State Capitol in downtown Olympia can be seen against the lower end of Puget Sound in the distance.

AUTHOR COLLECTION

Leopold became one of Butte's leading citizens and served a couple of terms in the Montana legislature.

In 1889, both Washington and Montana territories were scheduled to enter the Union as states. With this in mind, officials from the two worked together to draft their respective state constitutions. In the course of his duties as a state official, Leopold Schmidt traveled to Washington's capitol in Olympia.

While in Washington, Schmidt discovered the natural artesian waters in the town of Tumwater, immediately south of Olympia. He had it tested and decided it was the perfect water for brewing, so he moved his family and

base of operations west. He bought property for the new brewery in Tumwater on the Deschutes River at Lower Tumwater Falls. He also bought the water rights.

In 1896, Schmidt opened the Capital Brewing Company and kegged the first brew on October 1. In 1902, the company was renamed as the Olympia Brewing Company. By now, Schmidt's beer was popular throughout the Northwest, especially in the growing metropolis of Seattle.

Schmidt's Centennial Brewery in Butte was sold to Henry Mueller in 1897. It closed permanently in 1918. The Olympia brewery survived past the end of the twentieth century. In

1906, Schmidt built a grand new brick brewery building on his Tumwater property. Although this building became the symbol of the Olympia Brewing Company, it was the actual Olympia brewery for only eight years.

As had been the case in Montana, Leopold Schmidt quickly became one of Washington's leading citizens. He started a number of business ventures beyond the brewery, including hotels.

When Leopold died in 1914, his son, Peter, took the helm of the company just as Prohibition swept the nation. At the state capitol, almost in the shadow of the Olympia Brewery, Washington's legislators were among the first to adopt Prohibition. In 1915, the company brewed soft drinks as the Olympia Beverage Company. Eventually Schmidt went into the fruit business and sold his new brewery building to a paper company.

In 1933, Prohibition was repealed and the Schmidt family restarted the Olympia Brewing Company. A new brewing plant was constructed upriver and a short walk south of the original brewery. The old building wasn't reacquired by the Schmidt family until 1965, and by then the purchase was purely for sentimental reasons. By this time, the post-Prohibition plant had been modernized and expanded, and the original brewery was no longer useful as a modern commercial brewing facility.

The vast Olympia Brewery, as viewed across Interstate 5 from Tumwater's South Second Avenue Southwest. BILL YENNE

The big stainless steel brew kettles lined the main floor of the Olympia Brewery in this view from the 1960s.
AUTHOR COLLECTION

To say that the Olympia Brewing Company was an important fixture in Tumwater is a profound understatement. The people of Tumwater set their watches to the brewery's steam whistle, which was audible throughout the town. The brewery was the city's largest employer and it routinely shared water from its wells with the city at no charge.

Through the years, Olympia gradually evolved as one of the Northwest's most popular beers and competed with the products of the Blitz-Weinhard Brewery in Portland to the south and of Rainier Brewing in Seattle to the north. Olympia was marketed in California and exported to the Pacific. The brand's impact was so widespread that by the 1960s, "Oly" was referred to as the "national beer of Montana," even though it was an out-of-state brand and Montana had important commercial breweries within the state until nearly the end of the decade.

In small lettering at the top of the labels, Olympia identified its beer as being of the "Pale Export Type." The term *export* as a beer style originated during the nineteenth century in Dortmund, Germany. It was applied to a type of Dortmunder lager that was designed to withstand the rigors of travel by having more hops than comparable lagers. In a technical sense, it was like a bottom-fermented cousin to Britain's India Pale Ale. Olympia clearly had in mind that its lager would be exported, at least throughout the states of the Pacific Northwest and Mountain West.

During the 1960s, Oly had a tremendous presence in California as homegrown brands such as Acme and Lucky Lager faded. Olympia had a 24 percent market share in the Golden State during that decade.

This is the heart of the Olympia Brewery complex as viewed from Custer Way. A brand of beer that, for decades, flowed into a vast distribution network that spread eastward for hundreds of miles was brewed from within these walls. BILL YENNE

The familiar waterfall and horseshoe trademark was widely seen, and it was hard to find a tavern in the Northwest or Mountain West that didn't have an illuminated Oly waterfall bar sign. Few supermarkets in the West did not stock six-packs of the familiar short-necked, brown Olympia bottles known as stubbies. Between 1963 and the peak year of 1974, production at the Tumwater brewery increased from 2 million to 4.3 million barrels annually.

By the 1970s, an epidemic of consolidations gripped the American brewing industry and many large independent brewers acquired others of their kind or were acquired by them. For Olympia, it was the former. The company took possession of two companies, which were major regional icons at the time. In 1975, Olympia acquired the Theodore Hamm Brewing Company of St. Paul, Minnesota, and a year later, Olympia

took possession of the Lone Star Brewing Company in San Antonio, the "National beer of Texas." These acquisitions gave Olympia access to additional markets, and by 1982, the brand was available in 33 states.

In 1983, it was time for the acquisition tables to be turned. In what Olympia President Robert Schmidt described as an unfriendly takeover offer, Pabst Brewing of Milwaukee bought 49 percent of Olympia's outstanding stock and precipitated a sale of the Olympia Brewing Company to Pabst. At the same time, Leopold Schmidt's mansion was donated to the Olympia Tumwater Foundation, a nonprofit scholarship organization.

In the meantime, as Olympia had moved into Texas and Minnesota, brewing-industry consolidator Paul Kalmanovitz moved about the country and added brewing companies to his portfolio of S&P Holdings. In 1985, he acquired Pabst, the Olympia brand name, the big Tumwater brewery, and the rights to 6.56 million gallons of artesian water per day.

Kalmanovitz had a reputation for closing the breweries he acquired and slashing jobs, but the Tumwater plant was so modern and efficient that it became the crown jewel of his empire. Hamm's, the beer from the Land of Sky Blue Waters (Minnesota), was now brewed with the famous artesian water of Tumwater.

In 1990, the U.S. brewing industry underwent what some refer to as the "final consolidation." In 1996, industry giant G. Heileman was acquired by another mega-brewer, Stroh Brewing. In 1999, Stroh closed its doors and sold its brands, including the former Heileman properties, to Pabst. In the process, Pabst sold the venerable Hamm's brand and the big Tumwater brewery to the Miller Brewing Company.

The final consolidation left the Tumwater facility as the largest brewery in the Northwest. Its two biggest rivals—the Rainier Brewery in

Seattle and the Blitz-Weinhard Brewery in Portland—were Heileman properties that were passed to Stroh and closed in 1999.

In October 1999, Miller announced that it intended to invest $10 million to modernize and increase the production capacity at the 98-acre Tumwater complex. One of the first steps was to remove the Olympia sign from the brewery. While Miller assumed control of the brewery, the Olympia brand remained part of the Pabst portfolio. Ironically, because of Pabst closing all of its breweries and contracting all of its production, it contracted with Miller to brew Olympia. Olympia continued to be brewed at the original source in Tumwater, even though the brand and brewery were owned separately.

Despite the demise of the signature name, it seemed the brewery itself would have a secure future. Miller announced intentions to construct facilities that would more than double the plant's million-barrel annual output. However, the seeds of its demise had already been sewn in an intrigue involving the very thing upon which it had been founded—the water.

In 1982, the Schmidt family signed a 20-year wastewater treatment contract with the LOTT Wastewater Alliance. The acronym stood for the area that the alliance served, the cities of Lacey, Olympia, and Tumwater, and Thurston County. In January 2000, Miller announced it wanted to manage wastewater from the brewery and sell the unused capacity back to LOTT. A disagreement ensued that resulted in the planned expansion being put on hold. Thirteen months later, Miller and LOTT agreed to disconnect the brewery from the LOTT system, but in November 2001, the Washington Department of Ecology denied Miller a permit to discharge its own treated wastewater.

Six months later, in May 2002, it was announced that London-based South African Breweries (SAB) agreed to buy Miller Brewing Company from the Philip Morris Company. The new parent company, called SABMiller, became the second-largest brewing company in the world after Anheuser-Busch.

In January 2003, SABMiller announced that the Tumwater brewery closed. The reason was that the company could not justify the cost of its operations. Several days later, the LOTT Wastewater Alliance and the city of Tumwater formally

While many breweries picture dramatic natural landmarks on their labels, the waterfall on the Olympia label was a real waterfall that was literally at the brewery! Visible from the brewery's hospitality room, it was the icon of Tumwater's famous beverage. Note the bridge that can be seen on the labels. BILL YENNE

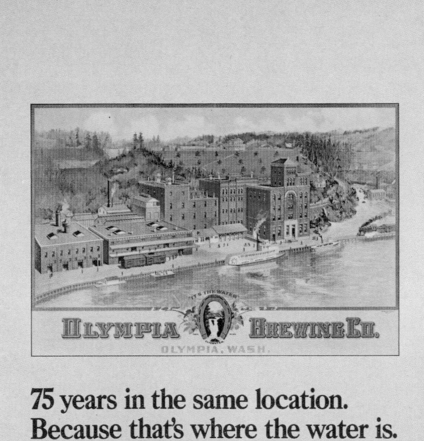

75 years in the same location. Because that's where the water is.

They grow the finest hops and malting barley
just over the mountain from here.
But that's not why we built our original brewery here.
Or our new, bigger brewery right up the hill.
We did it because of the water. The water from our
artesian wells. The naturally-perfect brewing water
that sets Olympia apart from every other beer.

It's the Water that Makes it Olympia

This two-page ad for Olympia from 1971 contains an inset picture of the original Olympia Brewery. The original facility was located only a tenth of a mile north of the main brewery and was sold in 1915 on the eve of Prohibition. It was reacquired by the Schmidt family 50 years later. AUTHOR COLLECTION

Stop in and help us celebrate 75 years in the same location. Olympia Brewing Company, Tumwater, Washington. 8:00 to 4:30 every day. *Oly**

99

At home in libraries as well as taverns, the lighted bar clocks with the legendary Olympia waterfall and horseshoe trademark was once common in nearly every village and hamlet in the Northwest.

BILL YENNE

When Pabst took control of Olympia in 1983, the label changed. The waterfall and horseshoe remained, albeit in simplified form, and it didn't have the silhouetted lines of evergreens. *AUTHOR COLLECTION*

The Olympia Light label that was introduced in the Pabst era drastically de-emphasized the waterfall and horseshoe trademark. At least the Olympia brand was still brewed at Tumwater for a while. *AUTHOR COLLECTION*

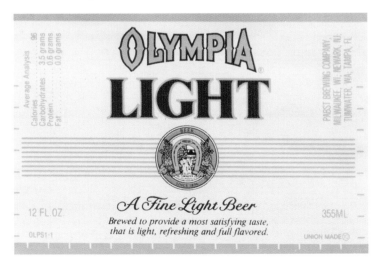

This historic marker is adjacent to Capitol Boulevard, where the thoroughfare cuts through the heart of the Olympia Brewing Company complex in Tumwater. The sign says it all. It really *was* the water! *BILL YENNE*

rescinded the February 2001 sewer service contract with the brewery, but the closure date was already set.

When Tumwater closed, the Redhook Ale Brewery of suburban Seattle became the largest brewery in the Northwest. Redhook had brewed 225,000 barrels in 2002, compared to 1.7 million at Tumwater.

The last of the famous stubbies came off the Tumwater bottle line on May 27, 2003, and the factory whistle sounded for the last time at 5:00 p.m. on June 20. The whistle was then donated to the city of Tumwater, moved to the Tumwater Valley Municipal Golf Course, and used on July 4 to herald the annual fireworks show.

The Tumwater brewery officially closed on June 26, 2003. The artesian water that Leopold Schmidt had discovered a century before still flowed, but it flowed untapped for brewing beer.

This is the classic Pabst Blue Ribbon label as it appeared in the 1980s. The red stripe was added to the blue ribbon in April 1958 when Pabst calculated that 100 million barrels of beer had been brewed since Jacob Best had started the Empire Brewery in Milwaukee in 1844. The red stripe is still with the blue ribbon today. AUTHOR COLLECTION

CHAPTER 9

Pabst Blue Ribbon

IF THEY HAD DECIDED to put brewery presidents instead of American presidents on Mount Rushmore, few men would seem more appropriate carved in solid granite than Captain Frederick Pabst, who presided over the largest brewery in America at the turn of the twentieth century.

Pabst Brewery.   Milwaukee, Wis.

The massive Pabst Brewery on Chestnut Street Hill in Milwaukee was one of Milwaukee's largest industrial sites and was the largest brewery in America by the end of the nineteenth century. *AUTHOR COLLECTION*

Pabst was the central casting image of a nineteenth-century American captain of industry, and he was a real captain. After plying the trade of a Great Lakes steamboat skipper, Pabst went ashore in 1859 and married Maria Best, the daughter of Phillip Best, a Milwaukee brewer. As sons-in-law often did in those days, Pabst took over the brewery.

Maria's grandfather, Jacob Best, a German immigrant from Mettenheim, founded the Empire Brewery on Chestnut Street in Milwaukee in 1844. Jacob's sons Charles and Phillip were the men who helped "make Milwaukee famous." Phillip and his brother Jacob Jr. took over the family business in 1853, and Charles started the company that evolved into Miller Brewing.

In 1860, Phillip became the sole owner of his dad's brewery, and the company was renamed the Phillip Best Company. Phillip's daughters had each married a young man with an interest in the brewing industry—Emil Schandien and Captain Frederick Pabst.

When Phillip Best retired in 1864, he placed his sons-in-law in charge of the company that he inherited from his father. By now, the corporate family tree that began two decades earlier with Jacob Best Sr. included

Captain Frederick Pabst was a Great Lakes steamboat skipper who became acquainted with Milwaukee brewer Phillip Best, who occasionally booked passage on Pabst's vessel, the Huron. The captain eventually married Best's daughter and took over the brewery. The rest, as they say, is brewing history. *BILL YENNE*

ENTRANCE TO PABST PARK, MILWAUKEE, WIS.

Both Captain Pabst and Joseph Schlitz created public parks in Milwaukee that were named after themselves. With its bandstands and beer garden, Pabst Park was a popular gathering place. Pabst Park was 8 acres and contained the Katzenjammer *fun house* and a roller coaster nearly 3 miles long.
AUTHOR COLLECTION

three of the principal names in Milwaukee brewing history: Best, Miller, and Pabst. Schandien passed away in 1888, and in 1889, Pabst took sole control of the company and renamed it Pabst Brewing.

With Captain Pabst's hand at the throttle, the Philip Best Company became the largest brewery in Milwaukee by the 1870s, second only to George Ehret's massive New York City company. However, the Captain didn't remain second for long.

By 1893, Pabst Brewing was the largest brewery in U.S. history and the first American brewer to exceed a million barrels of production annually. With Miller Brewing perpetually in third place locally, Pabst's biggest Milwaukee rival was Joseph Schlitz. Despite the Schlitz

slogan, Pabst always figured that he, not Schlitz, had made Milwaukee famous.

Captain Pabst became one of Milwaukee's most prominent citizens and was not shy about showing off his wealth. He acquired the Nunnemacher Opera House and renamed it for himself, and he commissioned George Bowman Ferry, a famous architect, to design a Flemish Renaissance Revival mansion for him on Milwaukee's Grand Avenue. The home took two years to complete and opened in 1892, wired for electricity and with plumbing for nine bathrooms.

Pabst cast his distribution network far and wide, from the farms and cities of the upper Midwest to the sparsely populated Plains and West. In 1899, he audaciously exported into New

At the turn of the twentieth century, before Prohibition, Pabst and other brewers marketed malt extract. It was a good source of fiber and a good thing to have around for brewing your own beer. At the time, the temperance movement was gathering steam and brewing companies wanted to position themselves as purveyors of healthy dietary products as well as intoxicating beverages. AUTHOR COLLECTION

In this beautifully illustrated 1896 ad, consumers were invited to win back their health with Pabst malt extract. It not only helped you sleep, it brought you strength. AUTHOR COLLECTION

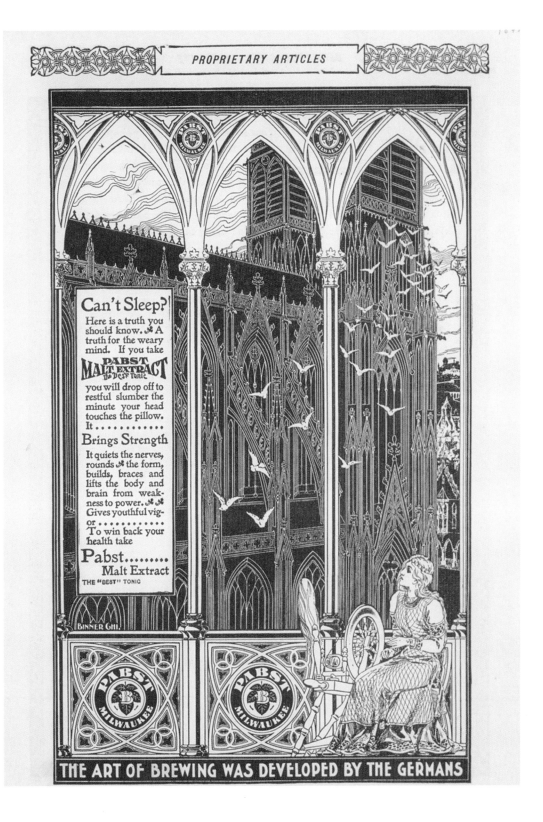

York City, where the local brewers had a volume unmatched anywhere but Milwaukee. He even opened a Pabst Hotel in New York.

With his characteristic flair for the dramatic, the Captain introduced the trademark that distinguished the Pabst flagship brand from all others. Mass production of bottled beer was relatively new, and the Captain went a step further to make his beer stand out. In 1882, Pabst began tying blue silk ribbons around bottles of Pabst Select Beer to identify the product in the minds of consumers as a first-place winner. In fact, it was a prize winner and brought home medals from the International Exposition in Paris in 1878 and the Chicago World's Fair in 1893.

The phrase "Blue Ribbon" was placed on Pabst bottles in 1895, where it remained through the turns of two centuries. In 1898, Pabst Select Beer was officially renamed Pabst Blue Ribbon Beer. The ribbon was such a popular gimmick that it spawned trademark infringement. Early in the twentieth century, Pabst went to court with the Storz Brewing Company when the Omaha upstart tied blue ribbons on its bottles. Pabst won.

Amazingly, the labor-intensive practice of hand-tying the silk ribbons onto the bottles continued until 1916. It took World War I and a shortage of silk on the world market to finally curtail the long-standing practice.

The Captain didn't live to see Prohibition descend upon his industry. When he passed away on New Year's Day in 1904, Pabst Brewing was at the

In the good old days, magazine ads were not a fast slogan or two, but short stories. The Binner advertising agency created this tale of a brave young woman going west to the gold fields of California with the 49ers. The miners were happy that she brought along her malt extract. With a little yeast and time, it restored their spirits. Pabst malt extract was known as the Best tonic because the brewery was started by Jacob Best. Note his initial at the center of the logo. AUTHOR COLLECTION

PERFECTION IN BREWING IS REACHED IN AMERICA

MAY FLOWER

PABST MILWAUKEE

BINNER CHICAGO

MOTHERS' MILK.

A young mother, flushed with perfect health and strength, said as she exhibited, with pride her baby, "I must confess that my present health and the almost phenomenal development and good health of baby are due to the use of

PABST MALT EXTRACT,
The "Best" Tonic.

The necessity of feeding the child was such a tax on me at first that I became nervous, weak and exhausted. "Best" Tonic was recommended. I took it and began to build at once. Baby began to show the effects within a week. I continued its use for months, until I went out into the country and neglected to take my tonic with me. I lost fifteen pounds in six weeks and could scarcely feed baby. Since returning, some three weeks ago, I have again been taking "Best" Tonic. I have gained six pounds and the little one is again progressing. Just think, he is nineteen months old, weighs 32 pounds, and I have not weaned him yet."

Let every mother apply this to her own experience and at least give The "Best" Tonic a trial. If not for her own sake, for that of her child. Let her provide for baby as nature says every mother should

According to Edward Winslow in Mourt's Relation: A Journal of the Pilgrims at Plymouth, *beer traveled to America aboard the Mayflower in 1620. In this ad from the late 1890s, Pabst suggests that malt extract could—or should—have been aboard as well.*
AUTHOR COLLECTION

peak of its power. It was still the largest in the nation, and Pabst Blue Ribbon was a household name from Chicago to New York City.

Frederick Jr. and his brother, Gustav, took over the company as it sailed into the rough and uncharted waters of the early twentieth century and Prohibition. Frederick Jr. retired as chairman of the Pabst board of directors in 1954.

BLUE RIBBON IS BEST

NORTH, East, South, West—wherever you go, Pabst Blue Ribbon is acknowledged the finest of beers. Its precision brewing gives you the essence of choice malt brought to full strength with the appetizing savor of fragrant hops. If you want the perfect beer, order Blue Ribbon, and make sure you get it. It's the nation's standing order for beer at its best.

PABST BLUE RIBBON BEER

The waiter pours a couple of Pabst Blue Ribbons for passengers in a railway dining car in 1934. Less than a year after Prohibition was repealed, the brand, along with its ribbon, was back. The tagline noted the Pabst sponsorship of the Ben Bernie musical variety show on NBC radio. Bernie was a popular band leader during the Jazz Age. AUTHOR COLLECTION

I'll say "33 to 1" wins at the 19th hole!

BLENDED 33 TIMES TO MAKE ONE GREAT BEER !

Try Pabst Blue Ribbon and Prove it

The notion of blending the brews from various kettles was an oblique way of touting the fact that the massive brewhouse in Milwaukee had 33 brew kettles. In 1940, Pabst used a ribbon on bottles of Pabst Blue Ribbon again, but it was short-lived after World War II began. AUTHOR COLLECTION

After the Captain died, ownership of the mansion was transferred to the Archdiocese of Milwaukee. It was the residence of the archbishop for seven decades before it was opened as a museum in 1978.

When Prohibition arrived in 1920, Pabst Brewing dropped the word *brewing* from the corporate name and reorganized as a producer of soft drinks, malt extract, and the nonalcoholic Pablo. The firm also marketed processed cheese that was made at the Pabst Farms in rural Wisconsin.

When Prohibition ended in 1933, the company reintroduced Pabst Blue Ribbon Beer, along with the actual cloth ribbon, and the beer quickly resumed its position of prominence among consumers. In 1933, to meet demand in the early years after the repeal, Pabst purchased the Premier Malt Products company, a Prohibition-era start-up in Peoria Heights, Illinois. With this, the official corporate name was the Premier-Pabst Corporation. In 1938, the word *Premier* was dropped.

Pabst became a leader in technical innovation during the 1930s and was among the first to offer canned beer and the new, easy-to-use metal keg. The canned beer was marketed as Pabst Export Beer. The name Pabst Blue Ribbon was reserved for the bottled product until the end of the decade.

For its post-Prohibition packaging, Pabst reintroduced the cloth ribbon, but it was permanently phased out by World War II. When the Pabst Blue

Ribbon name was introduced on canned beer in the late 1930s, the ribbon was pictured on the cans, but not on the bottle labels. It appeared on the neck bands of bottles during the late 1940s because it had been around the neck where the cloth ribbons had once been tied. By 1951, the blue ribbon had finally migrated to the main label, where it remained.

During World War II, Pabst ran its Blue Ribbon Town advertising campaign. In this series of ads, we met the leading citizens of an imaginary place where ribbons were alive with human heads. Here, the town doctor recites a poem about smashing the Axis and keeping Pabst Blue Ribbon on ice. AUTHOR COLLECTION

This is the Doctor of BLUE RIBBON TOWN
...whose Wartime Prescription is worth writing down

33 FINE BREWS BLENDED into One Great Beer

"This one's for me!"

Pabst Blue Ribbon
"IT'S BLENDED...IT'S SPLENDID!"

Copr. 1947, Pabst Brewing Company, Milwaukee, Wisc.

TUNE IN THE EDDIE CANTOR SHOW
EVERY THURSDAY NIGHT, OVER NBC

33 FINE BREWS BLENDED INTO ONE GREAT BEER

The party's over and the butler deserves a cold beer. After World War II, Pabst was not alone among the large American brewers that positioned its product as a beverage for high society.
AUTHOR COLLECTION

"Workman's Compensation!"

Pabst Blue Ribbon
"IT'S BLENDED...IT'S SPLENDID!"

33 FINE BREWS BLENDED INTO ONE GREAT BEER

Dad, who is doing a few chores around the house, is going to take a sip of Pabst Blue Ribbon before he hangs the picture. The ribbon was prominent in advertising, but not on the label at this time.
AUTHOR COLLECTION

Served at
"DUKE FARM," SOUTHAMPTON, L.I.
THE SUMMER ESTATE OF
Mr. and Mrs.
Angier Biddle Duke

...YOU HEAR IT EVERYWHERE...

"finest beer served
...anywhere!"
Your Taste will tell you why!

Internationally Famous *Pabst*
Blue Ribbon

33 FINE BREWS BLENDED INTO ONE GREAT BEER • Copr. 1949, Pabst Brewing Co., Milwaukee, Wisconsin

Even in the late 1940s, the Hamptons were home to the elite. Here, we visit Angier Biddle Duke, and his wife, the former Robin Chandler, sipping Pabst Blue Ribbon at their summer place in Southampton. Angier's family was responsible for Duke University, and he later served as ambassador to Spain, Denmark, and Morocco and was a member of the Council on Foreign Relations. AUTHOR COLLECTION

Served in the Connecticut Home of
Miss Gladys Swarthout
and her husband
Mr. Frank Chapman

HOLIDAY for MISS SWARTHOUT, and You

Pabst
Blue Ribbon

33 FINE BREWS BLENDED INTO ONE GREAT BEER

The legendary opera diva, Gladys Swarthout, relaxed with her husband and a couple of Pabst Blue Ribbons at their home in Connecticut. Swarthout debuted at the Chicago Civic Opera and had a 16-year career with the Metropolitan Opera in New York City. In 1949, Pabst advertising featured a series that showed society's elite enjoying the product.
AUTHOR COLLECTION

By the eve of World War II, the American beer business was better than ever, and the end of the war led to a period of unprecedented prosperity. It also led to the dawn of the era of the great national breweries. The first generation of great national breweries emerged in the 1940s and included Anheuser-Busch, Schlitz, and Pabst. These companies met increasing demand though expansion, and expanded through acquisition. Because all three were located in the middle of the United States, the obvious strategic move was to set up

SERVED TO
Mr. & Mrs. Lawrence Tibbett
ABOARD THE
S. S. Brazil
MOORE-McCORMACK LUXURY LINER

YOU HEAR IT EVERYWHERE
..."finest beer served
anywhere!"

THE REASON:
33 FINE BREWS BLENDED INTO ONE GREAT BEER

Internationally
Famous *Pabst*
Blue Ribbon

Pabst, Blue Ribbon, and the representation of a blue ribbon, are the registered trade-marks of Pabst Brewing Company. Copr. 1949, Pabst Brewing Co., Milwaukee, Wisconsin

By 1949, Pabst Blue Ribbon seems to have been the beer of choice at New York City's Metropolitan Opera. Legendary baritone Lawrence Tibbett, seen here vacationing aboard the SS Brazil luxury liner, was beginning his last season at the Met in the role of Prince Ivan Khovansky in Khovanschina when this ad appeared. He also had a film career during the 1930s and a recording career that continued into the 1950s. AUTHOR COLLECTION

brewing operations on both coasts.

Pabst actually got into the New York market before Schlitz or Anheuser-Busch thanks to the purchase of the Hoffman Beverage Company of Newark in 1946. Acquiring the 12-year-old New Jersey brewer placed Pabst's operations within the heavily populated Northeast.

Seven years later, Pabst secured a foothold on the rapidly growing Pacific Coast with the purchase of the Los Angeles Brewing Company. The brewery was

famous for its popular Eastside and Mission brands. In 1958, Pabst bought the Blatz Brewery, one of its original Milwaukee rivals.

As with the other national brands, Pabst supported its expansion with a great deal of national print and radio advertising during the late 1940s. By the mid-1950s, television became an important element in the advertising mix. Much of the advertising portrayed Pabst Blue Ribbon as a sophisticated brew that was served to the carriage trade from silver platters by tuxedoed butlers. Captain Pabst would have smiled.

The quarter-century following World War II was generally a good time for Pabst. It never saw the number one spot among American brewers that it had enjoyed with the Captain's hand on the tiller, but Pabst remained among the top five American brewing companies longer than any other company other than Anheuser-Busch. The two were the only companies among that elite quintet in 1950, 1960, 1970, and 1980. Pabst's volume grew from 3.4 million barrels in 1950 to 4.7 million in 1960, 10 million in 1970, and an all-time peak of 18 million barrels in 1977.

By the 1970s, the "New South" was where marketers looked for an expanding economy, and Pabst opened a new plant in Perry, Georgia, in 1971. The town was even known briefly as Pabst, Georgia. In 1979, Pabst acquired another western brewing company, the Blitz Weinhard Brewing Company of Portland, Oregon, which had become a major regional player in the Northwest.

Much of Pabst's success in this era had been attributed to James Windham, who took over as Pabst's president in 1958, when the company acquired Milwaukee rival Blatz Brewing, which Windham had

By 1950, the emphasis
in beer advertising
shifted from the
upper crust to
sports heroes.
Tommy Heinrich was
an outfielder with
the New York
Yankees from 1937
through 1950. Here
he relives the team's
victory over
Brooklyn in the 1949
World Series that led
to his Athlete of the
Year award.

AUTHOR COLLECTION

The distinguished trophy
you see on the table was awarded
to Tommy Henrich January 19, 1950
as "Athlete of the Year."

Tommy Henrich, *Athlete-of-the-Year*...
showing his World Series home-run baseball while
enjoying that world-famous Pabst Blue Ribbon taste.

YOU HEAR IT EVERYWHERE...

"finest beer served
...anywhere!"

Your Taste will tell you why!

Internationally
Famous

Pabst
Blue Ribbon

TUNE IN "THE LIFE OF RILEY" starring WILLIAM BENDIX, every Friday night over NBC.

Copyright 1950, Pabst Brewing Company, Milwaukee, Wisconsin

headed. Windham served as president, and later chairman, of Pabst until his death in 1977.

Although the advertising after World War II had positioned Pabst Blue Ribbon as a very stylish and sophisticated beverage, it was recast as a working class beer in the 1970s. The decade was one of outlaw country music, and Pabst Blue Ribbon was embraced for this genre by the songwriting team of Chuck Neese, Bob McDill, and Wayland Holyfield. In 1973, Johnny Russell had his first top-five hit with his song "Rednecks, White Socks, and Blue Ribbon Beer." "There's no place that I'd rather be than right here," Russell intoned, "with my redneck, white socks, and blue ribbon beer."

If the late 1940s and 1950s saw the rise of the great national brewers, the period three decades later was the era of consolidation. For Pabst, the Blitz-Weinhard acquisition was just the beginning. Theodore Hamm Brewery of St. Paul was acquired by Olympia Brewing of Tumwater, Washington, in 1975, but Pabst bought them both in 1983. Also in 1983, two years after Stroh Brewing bought Schlitz, Pabst bought the former Schlitz expansion brewery in Tampa, Florida. During the same year, Pabst sold both Blitz-Weinhard and its Perry, Georgia, expansion brewery to Heileman Brewing. Meanwhile, the old Premier-Pabst facility in Peoria Heights was closed for good.

With the disappearance of Schlitz as an independent brand, it was clear that no one was immune from the consolidation. Even Pabst itself was

For Christmas 1951, Pabst put the ribbon on the primary bottle label of Pabst Blue Ribbon. Although the type style and treatment were altered several times over the decades, this general configuration remained through the turn of the century. AUTHOR COLLECTION

In this 1958 ad, both the artist and his model are enjoying a "perfect" pilsner glass of Pabst Blue Ribbon. In the tagline, Pabst mentions two other products that received less notoriety than the flagship product. Old Tankard had been around since before World War II, and Andeker was a lesser Pabst brand until the 1980s.

AUTHOR COLLECTION

A lineup of Pabst brewery trucks, seen here in 1954, did an advertising tie-in for the film The Human Jungle, *which starred Gary Merrill and Jan Sterling.* AUTHOR COLLECTION

seen by many as ripe for an outside takeover. In 1985, Paul Kalmanovitz paid $63 million to add Pabst to the portfolio of his S&P holding company. Under Kalmanovitz, Pabst's flagship brewery in Milwaukee was closed and the huge art collection started by Captain Pabst was shipped to California. All advertising for Pabst Blue Ribbon was terminated, and the Tampa facility was sold to Stroh Brewing.

When Kalmanovitz died in 1988, the obituary for Pabst was already written and ready to run. However, Lutz Issleib, the new Pabst president, wanted to turn the company around. This effort would be part of a new round of consolidation in the 1990s.

In 1996, Stroh Brewing, America's third-largest brewing company, bought number five Heileman. Within a few years of swallowing Heileman, the cachet of Stroh's large portfolio of brands had faded. A major part of the company's business was contract-brewing for the likes of Boston Beer Company, purveyors of the fast-growing Samuel Adams brand, and Pabst.

When Jim Koch of Boston Beer decided to pull out of Stroh and move to Miller Brewing in 1999, John Stroh III announced that the Stroh family

In 1989, America's large mass market brewing companies longed for a new product, and dry beer was born. Low in malt content and flavor-neutral, dry beers were popular for a short time. Nevertheless, all the major brewers leapt on the bandwagon. Pabst omitted the red stripe for the label of its dry product.

The Pabst Extra Light product didn't mention a blue ribbon, but brought the "B for Best" insignia to the forefront. These labels (above, below) from the early and late 1980s showed the consolidation of the Pabst portfolio of breweries through the decades. By the end of the decade, only the Milwaukee flagship and the Olympia site in Tumwater remained.

When Pabst introduced the light version of Pabst Blue Ribbon, the label design was essentially the same as for the standard Pabst Blue Ribbon, complete with ribbon and red stripe.

Pabst attempted to use the company name on a nonalcoholic product in the 1980s. The thing pictured behind the "NA" is intended to be a blue ribbon, but it could be interpreted as a can opener. AUTHOR COLLECTION

Pabst paid tribute to the original founder of the company during the 1980s with a limited-release product called Jacob Best Premium Light. No expense or time had been spared to brew a beer worthy of his name.
AUTHOR COLLECTION

Andeker, earlier called "Andeker of America" or "Andeker Draught Supreme," was a product name used off and on after World War II by Pabst for lagers positioned in the premium beer market. This particular label featured a nonstandard "B for Best" logo and was from the mid-1980s.
AUTHOR COLLECTION

would pull the plug on the family business a year short of its 150th birthday. The Stroh family sold its Stroh and Heileman brands to Miller and Pabst. In this massive industry shuffle, Miller acquired the Blitz-Weinhard brands that Pabst sold to Heileman, but Pabst acquired the rest of the surviving former Heileman and Stroh brand names. Meanwhile, Pabst sold the Hamm's and Olympia brands that it had owned since 1983 to Miller.

Pabst consolidated its actual brewing operations to San Antonio, Texas, where the Pearl Brewing facility had been added to the S&P portfolio in 1988. At the end of 2002, Pabst entirely ceased to brew beer. At the beginning of 2003, the Pearl plant was sold and Pabst became a virtual brewer. All of the brands in the Pabst portfolio were contract-brewed by other companies.

Despite this turn of events, the new virtual brewer held a commanding position in the industry. In terms of sales at the turn of the century, only Anheuser-Busch, Miller, and Coors had greater volume than the Pabst brands. Pabst, the biggest name at the beginning of the twentieth century, had faded to near obscurity in the 1990s but surged back to the number four position as the century ended.

The retro styling of this attractive label looked like it was borrowed from early twentieth-century Rainier label artwork, but it was actually produced in the 1980s. *AUTHOR COLLECTION*

CHAPTER 10

Rainier

THE RAINIER STORY is one of a pioneer city and an entrepreneurial family of legendary proportions. Seattle, the major metropolis of the Pacific Northwest, grew up fast as a center of the lumbering and fishing industries. The loggers and fishermen grew thirsty, and the brewing industry naturally followed. A. B. Rabbeson started Seattle's first commercial brewery, Washington Brewery, in 1854.

This was 15 years before the city was officially incorporated and 35 years before Washington became a state.

Rabbeson's establishment became the Seattle Brewery in 1872, which survived until 1888. By this time, especially during the 1880s, a number of other brewers came on the scene. The operation begun by John Kopp and Andrew Hemrich in 1883 became Seattle Brewing and Malting. The company was best known as "the House of Hemrich" and

swallowed up five other Seattle breweries between 1892 and 1904. In the process, the company acquired the brand name Rainier, which had been used in Seattle as early as 1878.

The brand name was so ubiquitous that many people once subscribed to the urban legend that the snowcapped 14,410-foot mountain that is visible from Seattle was named after the beer! In fact, British Captain George Vancouver had named the Cascade Range volcanic peak after Admiral Peter

This turn-of-the-century photograph, taken at Seattle Brewing and Malting, shows the Rainier brand name already in use. Born in 1892 through a consolidation of five smaller companies, the company folded in 1915. After Prohibition, the Sicks bought the company, but they didn't have full use of the Rainier brand name until 1940. AUTHOR COLLECTION

Rainier in 1792. Of course, the point that the two western Washington icons shared the name did not hurt sales of the beer.

Although he did not coin the brand name, Emil G. Sick was the architect of its rise to fame. Sick was born in Tacoma in 1894 and was the son of Fritz Sick, a pioneer brewery owner with an international chain of breweries. Born in Freiburg, Germany, Fritz Sick trained as a coppersmith and immigrated to America in 1883 at the age of 24. He found employment in the brewing trade, where there was a high demand for copper work. Eventually, he moved to western Canada and established small breweries in Fernie and Trail, British Columbia.

In 1901, Fritz Sick started the Lethbridge Brewing and Malting Company in Lethbridge, Alberta. By 1911, he produced 40,000 barrels of beer annually under the name Alberta Pride. By this time, the dark specter of Prohibition loomed on the horizon in Canada and the United States. In Canada, the cruel experiment arrived earlier but didn't last as long and varied from province to province. Prohibition was enacted in the United

Looking a bit worse for wear late in the twentieth century, the big brick smokestack at Sick's Seattle Brewing and Malting presided over a half-century of legendary beer production in the Emerald City. BILL YENNE

States in 1920 and wasn't repealed until 1933. In Alberta, it went into effect in 1916, but it lasted only until 1923.

Fritz Sick survived in Lethbridge and produced soft drinks. When Prohibition faded, he promptly expanded his brewing empire. He acquired a brewery in Regina, Saskatchewan, in 1923 and another in Edmonton, Alberta, four years later. In 1930, he added another in Vancouver, British Columbia, to his portfolio. By this time, Fritz turned the reins of the family business over to Emil.

When Prohibition ended in the United States in 1933, Fritz and Emil came south to acquire Seattle Brewing and Malting, which had not yet resumed production of beer. The Rainier brand name was proudly relaunched, although the Sicks didn't acquire full rights to the brand until 1940. In 1935, without having actually started brewing at the Seattle Brewing and Malting site, they acquired Century Brewing, which began on Seattle's Airport Way in 1933. The Sick headquarters was moved from Lethbridge to the Airport Way site in Seattle, which was renamed Sick's Seattle Brewing and Malting.

In the meantime, Rainier was also being brewed in San Francisco. A Rainier brewery opened on Bryant Street in 1916. During the next decade, the facility produced a variety of nonalcoholic products under a variety of names, including Tacoma Brewing and Pacific Products. It emerged from Prohibition as Rainier Brewing and remained as such until the Theodore Hamm Brewing acquired it in 1953.

Emil Sick was an empire builder like his father. He set out to add to the chain his father had built in Canada through parallel acquisitions across the northern tier of the United States. In 1940, he bought the Spokane Brewery, across the state in the city of the same name, which had been started by Galland Burke in 1892. It was renamed Sick's Rainier Brewery of Spokane in 1958. In 1943, Emil acquired the Salem Brewery in Oregon's state

capital, which had been started by Samuel Adolph in 1874.

In 1944, Emil Sick bought two breweries in Montana, just across the border from Alberta. These were Missoula Brewing, which had been started by George Gerber in 1874, and Great Falls Breweries, which originated in 1895 as American Brewing. With the Missoula and Great Falls acquisitions, Sick took possession of the two most prominent brand names in Montana: Highlander and Great Falls Select. Highlander was so prominent that it was also brewed at the Rainier plant in Seattle.

Fritz Sick died in 1945 at the age of 85 and saw his modest chain of breweries evolve into a multinational empire. At the time, the Sick family is said to have had the largest number of breweries under a single ownership in the world.

Before Fritz Sick reached Seattle, he sought his fortune in Lethbridge, Alberta. He started Sick's Lethbridge Brewing and Malting in 1901 and kept the location as his headquarters for three decades as he expanded his empire south and west. The original brand name in Lethbridge was Alberta Pride, but the later flagship brand was Lethbridge Beer, better known as Bridge. Molson acquired the facility in 1959. *MOLSON COLLECTION, PUBLIC ARCHIVES OF CANADA, VIA AUTHOR COLLECTION*

This is the classic mid-twentieth-century Rainier label from Sick's Seattle Brewing and Malting. Mount Rainier and the 6 Sicks' Symbol of Quality, a pun on the Sick family name, were used in packaging and promotion. *AUTHOR COLLECTION*

Artifacts revealed by the retreating snowdrifts as spring comes to eastern Montana include this Great Falls Select can. Emil Sick acquired Great Falls Breweries in 1944 and held them for several years before the company went independent. The plant wound up in the Blitz-Weinhard portfolio and was closed for good in 1968. BILL YENNE

In the meantime, Emil Sick had become one of Seattle's leading citizens. He founded the King County Blood Bank, served as chairman for the March of Dimes, and was president of the Seattle Chamber of Commerce.

As with Jacob Ruppert in New York City, Sick owned the major brewery in town, as well as the major baseball team. Ruppert owned the New York Yankees from 1915 until his death in 1939. Emil Sick owned the Seattle Rainiers when that Pacific Coast League's players had a higher pay scale than the American and National leagues.

Emil Sick bought the Seattle Indians baseball franchise at the end of 1937. By the time the first pitch was thrown in the 1938 season, they were the Seattle Rainiers, although they were generally known as "the Suds."

Sick built the team a new steel-and-concrete stadium at the corner of Rainier and McClelland streets to replace the old Dugdale Field, which burned down during a fireworks display in July 1932. The new ballpark, known as Sicks' Seattle Stadium, debuted in June 1938. Under Sick's ownership, the Rainiers won the Pacific Coast League pennant in 1939, 1940, and 1941.

In 1951, Sick hired Hall of Fame hitter Rogers Hornsby to manage the Rainiers. He stayed only one season, but he led the team to another pennant win. Through the years, the Rainiers included great players such as Fred Hutchinson, Jim Rivera, Bob Boyd, Lou Kretlow, Edo Vanni, Hal Turpin, Bill Lawrence, Jo Jo White, Bill Schuster, and "Kewpie" Dick Barrett. The team's greatest pitcher, Barrett, pitched a perfect game in 1948 at the age of 40.

In 1955, with Fred Hutchinson as manager, the Rainiers earned a fifth pennant. Five years later, Emil Sick sold the team to the Boston Red Sox as a Triple-A franchise. Sicks' Seattle Stadium survived until 1979, three years after the controversial Kingdome, the original home of the Seattle Mariners, was completed.

Emil Sick gradually divested himself of his brewing interests. In 1956, he sold a majority interest in Sick's Seattle Brewing and Malting to Molson Breweries Ltd., Canada's oldest and largest brewing concern. In turn, the Seattle-based entity was renamed Sick's Rainier Brewing Company. Over the next decade, the former Sick

Traditionally one of western Montana's signature brands, Highlander became part of Emil Sick's portfolio in 1944 when he acquired the Missoula Brewing Company. The brand was so popular west of the Rockies that Sick also brewed it in Seattle alongside Rainier. The brand ceased to exist in 1964. AUTHOR COLLECTION

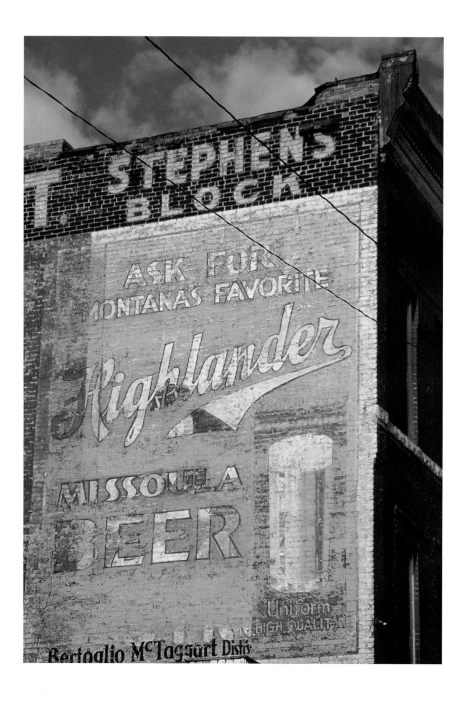

empire was gradually disassembled. The Sick name was officially dropped from the corporate appellation in 1970. Sick's Lethbridge Brewery was sold to Molson Western Breweries Ltd. in 1959. It survived for three decades until it was closed after the merger of Molson with Carling O'Keefe.

When Emil Sick died in 1964, his baseball team and Canadian brewery were gone, and his breweries in the United States were slipping away. The Salem brewery had ceased production in 1953, but the others continued until the 1960s, when the Sick's Breweries were heavily impacted by the market penetration of the national mega-brewers and the general consolidation within the industry. The Spokane brewery was closed in 1962, and the Highlander facility in Missoula followed in 1964, but the Highlander brand continued to be brewed in Seattle.

Although the former Sick empire was gone by the end of the 1960s, the Rainier name and the brewery in Seattle remained. The name still had a robust regional presence throughout the Northwest. The popularity of the product remained strong through clever advertising campaigns such as the memorable "Rainier Brewmaster," a stern individual with shaven head and handlebar mustache.

In the late 1970s, the G. Heileman Brewing Company of LaCrosse, Wisconsin, went west on a buying spree looking to add important regional brands to its portfolio. Heileman acquired Rainier in 1977 and

In 1970, the company name was changed from Sick's Rainier Brewing Company to Rainier Brewing Company. Molson Breweries Ltd. of Canada acquired the controlling interest from the family in 1956. AUTHOR COLLECTION

With bilingual labels, Molson marketed the Seattle-brewed products of their Rainier Brewing Company in Canada through the 1970s. The Rainier brand was sold to Heileman of LaCrosse, Wisconsin, in 1977. AUTHOR COLLECTION

Portland's Blitz-Weinhard in 1983. In 1987, Heileman itself was acquired by Alan Bond of Australia, whose holdings constituted one of the world's largest multinational companies, including the Swan Brewery and the Pittsburgh Brewing Company, which brewed Iron City, the signature brand of western Pennsylvania.

In the summer of 1996, Stroh acquired Heileman's five breweries, including the main Heileman plant in La Crosse, Wisconsin; Weinhard in Portland; and Rainier in Seattle. In 1999, Stroh closed most of the Heileman brewing plants, including the Rainier brewery on Airport Way in Seattle, sold its brands to the Pabst Brewing Company, and went out of business. The Airport Way facility was acquired by the Tully's Coffee Corporation.

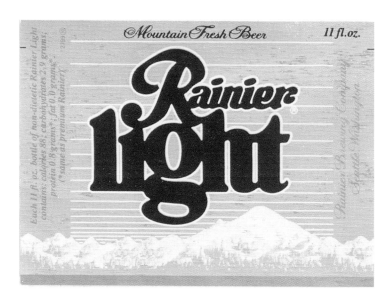

In the late 1970s, when all of the major American brewing companies began producing light variations on their flagship products, Rainier followed suit. AUTHOR COLLECTION

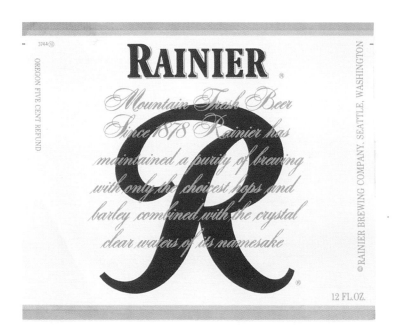

In the 1980s, the Rainier label was redesigned with a panel of text overlaying the signature red R. The picture of Mount Rainier was dropped in favor of a description of the mountain and its water. AUTHOR COLLECTION

The redesign of the Rainier label in the 1980s used a white background for the regular product and a silver foil background for the light variation. AUTHOR COLLECTION

This billboard in Spokane from 1995 shows how Rainier followed the industry's marketing trends. After the success of light beers, the industry sought new and ultimately short-lived variations on its basic product in the never-ending battle for market share. Dry beers were the fad, which were followed by ice beers. The latter were high-alcohol-content lagers created by crystallizing water, which freezes at a lower temperature than alcohol. *BILL YENNE*

During the 1930s and 1940s, Rainier produced ale and lager. By the 1960s, Rainier was one of the last of the old-line, big-city brewing companies to brew ale. The Old Stock name survived the sale to Molson and was used on Rainier Ale packaging until about 1973. *AUTHOR COLLECTION*

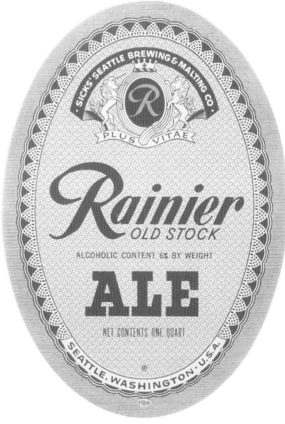

While lagers and light lagers remained the standard Rainier products, the brewery continued to brew ale well into the last years of the twentieth century. Before the microbrewery revolution changed the scene in the 1980s, Rainier Ale was the largest selling local ale in the Far West. *AUTHOR COLLECTION*

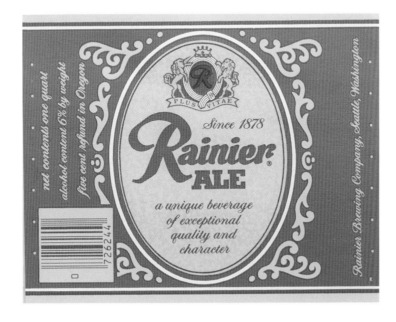

This twenty-first-century point-of-sale piece traces the Rheingold lineage to 1883, the year that Joseph, Charles, and Henry Liebmann first introduced the Rheingold brand to New York City. COURTESY OF TERRY LIEBMAN, RHEINGOLD BREWING COMPANY

CHAPTER 11

Rheingold

THE HISTORY OF BEER marketing is filled with unforgettable slogans and extraordinary campaigns, but the campaign used between 1940 and 1965 to market the Rheingold brand captured the imagination of its target audience like no other. The Miss Rheingold campaign was literally the talk of the town in America's largest metropolitan area for a quarter-century.

Eugenia "Jinx" Falkenburg had already appeared in a half-dozen films by age 20 when Philip Liebmann picked her to be the brewery's Miss Rheingold 1940. Her face launched one of the legendary advertising campaigns in American brewing history.
AUTHOR COLLECTION

Sonia Gover, Miss Rheingold 1943, relaxes with a fellow model on the set of a Rheingold photo shoot. The product being served is the brewery's flagship product, Extra Dry Lager. The dry appellation predated the industry's dry-beer fad by four decades. AUTHOR COLLECTION

After her year as Miss Rheingold, Jinx Falkenburg moved to Hollywood, where she starred in a dozen films through 1946. Here she is with Joe E. Brown, Walt Disney, and Charlie Ruggles. She co-hosted the Tex and Jinx show on radio and television with her husband, Tex McCrary. AUTHOR COLLECTION

When the Liebmann Breweries of Brooklyn nominated its six candidates for its annual Miss Rheingold title, the enthusiasm for the campaign rivaled that of a presidential election.

A century before there was a Miss Rheingold, the Liebmanns were a German immigrant brewing family who had been active brewers since 1837. Joseph, Charles, and Henry came to New York City from Bavaria in about 1850, and they sent for their father, Samuel, soon after. Known as S. Liebmann's Sons, the family brewery began in 1854 on Meserole Street in the Williamsburg section of Brooklyn. In 1855, the Liebmanns relocated their operation to the corner of Forrest and Bremen streets in Bushwick. The area was then part of Long Island City, but it was later incorporated into

Sonia Gover pulls a few strings for a Scottish lassie while promoting Rheingold's Ale. The label carried a bit of tartan plaid to identify the product as having a bit of a Highland flavor. AUTHOR COLLECTION

Brooklyn, which became a borough of New York City in 1898. Brooklyn was the de facto brewing capital of the entire region in the nineteenth century.

Samuel Liebmann's daughters married two beer-brewing brothers named Obermeyer. In 1868, David Obermeyer, along with brother-in-law Joseph Liebmann, opened shop nearby at Bremen and Noll streets, and started the Obermeyer and Liebmann Havana Brewery. The Obermeyer and Liebmann company operated independently from the other branch of the family business until they merged after the Prohibition was lifted. The relationship between the two family breweries is said to have been amicable.

In a unique cooperative arrangement, the three sons rotated the office of chief executive at S. Liebmann's Sons among themselves until after the turn of the century. The Liebmanns were leaders in technical innovation and were among the first brewers in Brooklyn to install a mechanical refrigeration system. Introduced in 1870, their unit was designed by the French inventor Ferdinand Carre and used liquid ammonia compression.

In 1920, when the dark cloud of Prohibition fell across the nation's great family breweries, the Liebmann company remained in business, produced near beer, and absorbed the

Obermeyer and Liebmann firm in 1924. When the company emerged from Prohibition in 1933 under the name Liebmann Breweries, Charles' sons, Julius and Alfred, took up the reins of management. Subsequently, Alfred's son Philip was the fourth-generation Liebmann to head the company.

In 1883, Joseph, Charles, and Henry Liebmann first introduced the Rheingold brand that became the Liebmann signature product. The name referenced German mythology and the legend of the enchanted cache of gold possessed by the Nibelung family. The tale was immortalized in a series of operas by German composer Richard Wagner called the *Ring des Nibelungen*. The first of these, *Das Rheingold*, was completed in 1854, the year that the Liebmanns started their brewery in America. During the coming decades, Rheingold evolved into one of the best-known brands in the New York City metropolitan area, and *Das Rheingold* was occasionally performed at New York City's Metropolitan Opera.

For this photo shoot, Miss Rheingold 1943 donned a uniform to support the war effort. The second Miss Rheingold elected by popular vote, Sonia Gover was the first to be chosen after the United States entered World War II. AUTHOR COLLECTION

Let it snow. Actually, the grass is green and the sleigh is a prop. On the set of a photo shoot in the summer of 1943, Sonia Gover pretends it's almost Christmas, and she's delivering barrels of lager to holiday revelers. AUTHOR COLLECTION

The Liebmann Breweries flourished in the 1930s and 1940s, but the years immediately after World War II were marked by a dramatic economic expansion and an increased demand for beer. The major New York City brewing companies expanded production, and in many cases, acquired smaller, existing companies. In 1947, Liebmann purchased the John Eichler Brewery on Third Avenue, which dated back to the Kolb Brewery that was constructed on the site in 1862. Aside from the Obermeyer and Liebmann merger, this was the first outside acquisition made by Liebmann since 1878, when Samuel Liebmann took over the recently closed J. P. Schoenewald Brewery in Brooklyn.

In 1950, Philip Liebmann, the company chief executive, added the John F. Trommer Brewery to the company's holdings. Founded in 1901 as the Orange Brewery, it was the only commercial brewing company that ever existed in Orange, New Jersey. In 1954, Philip Liebmann purchased the former Acme breweries in Los Angeles and San Francisco. This bold move made Liebmann the only one of the big New York City brewing companies to operate breweries in the West. However, this costly venture was terminated after four years.

Philip developed and launched an advertising campaign

that made the Rheingold brand name much more than the household word that it already was. During the 1930s, Liebmann advertising described Rheingold with the phrase, "That's good beer. . . ." It was a good advertising slogan, but not exceptional. What was needed was an exceptional advertising campaign.

One day in the latter part of 1939, Philip discussed the printing of some Rheingold advertising materials with Bob Wechsler. He lived near Philip and worked for Einson Freeman, the advertising agency that handled the Rheingold account. To demonstrate a particular printing process, Wechsler happened to have some printed photographs of Eugenia Lincoln Falkenburg, a young Spanish-born Chilean actress and model.

Best known by her nickname, Jinx, the 20-year-old Falkenburg had appeared in nine films since 1935—eight of them in the United States—and was already on her way to becoming one of the leading models in New York City. Philip Liebmann thought she would be a good addition to Rheingold advertising materials, and her agent was contacted. A Rheingold Girl had appeared in Liebmann advertising around 1911, but the concept had not been used since. Philip Liebmann decided that it was an idea worth reviving, and Jinx Falkenburg became the Rheingold Girl of 1940. The term *Miss Rheingold* was later introduced.

Francine Counihan was a runner-up for Miss Rheingold 1945 and went on to Hollywood. She was featured in the film Cover Girl *as the cover girl on* American Home. *Jinx Falkenburg also had a cameo in the picture.* AUTHOR COLLECTION

Rita Daigle, Miss Rheingold 1946, is dressed for the Easter Parade in an Easter bonnet, gloves, and a dress by Sophie of Sak's Fifth Avenue. The chicken is much more interested in the eggs than the parade. *AUTHOR COLLECTION*

By August 1945, the GIs started to come stateside from overseas, and what a dream it was to think of a couple of fried eggs, a picnic with Pat Boyd, and a cold Rheingold. *AUTHOR COLLECTION*

Spots were the fashion statement of choice for Pat Boyd and her dog as they stepped out in style in the first peacetime autumn that New Yorkers had seen since Ruth Ownbey had reigned as Miss Rheingold. *AUTHOR COLLECTION*

These six young women were selected from among hundreds who gathered at the Waldorf Astoria in 1945. By summer, voting took place at taverns and stores all over New York City. After the last votes were cast on August 31, one lucky woman won the $2,000 in war bonds and another grand in modeling fees. *AUTHOR COLLECTION*

Michaele Fallon, Miss Rheingold 1947, watered her plants with looking, but the folks at Liebmann had their eyes on the ball. the tagline notes, the brewery produced Rheingold McSorley's True Hearty Ale for McSorley's Old Ale House on West 7th S in Manhattan. This venerable institution celebrated its centen in 1954. *AUTHOR COLLECTION*

Always a straight shooter, Michaele Fallon displays her target with 10 pretty good hits after a day at the range on September 20, 1947. It was time for a beer, and what better beer than the Rheingold McSorley's True Hearty Ale? Unfortunately, McSorley's Old Ale House didn't admit women until 1970. *AUTHOR COLLECTION*

The dude ranch in the West was all the rage in the late 1940s, and Pat Quinlan, Miss Rheingold 1948, went all out. By now, there were 25,000 Rheingold dealers in greater New York. *AUTHOR COLLECTION*

In November 1949, Pat McElroy got into the autumn mood by taking in a football game. Her favorite team had a name beginning with the letter R, as did her favorite beer. What a coincidence! *AUTHOR COLLECTION*

Elise Gammon was ready for the magical Christmas 1951 ball with her bejeweled dress from Fira Benenson, her arctic fox fur by Harra, and her dry beer by Rheingold. *AUTHOR COLLECTION*

Anne Hogan was ready for spring. She'd hang out her birdhouse, then sit back with a cold Rheingold to watch the birds arrive. A great deal of the Rheingold photography was done in Beverly Hills, the base of operations for photographer Paul Hesse. *AUTHOR COLLECTION*

Dressed for the occasion in white gloves, Hillie Merritt, Miss Rheingold 1956, takes a trip to Coney Island. One wonders why such a lovely young lady is riding alone. Maybe the object was for a Rheingold fan to picture himself beside her. *AUTHOR COLLECTION*

An active Miss Rheingold was standard fare for summer advertising. Here, Nancy Woodruff sets out with her scooter in 1955 to work up a thirst for her favorite dry beer. AUTHOR COLLECTION

Duded up as a cowgirl, Hillie Merritt sets out on a picnic in a surrey with a fringe on top and a collie at her side. By 1956, the ads claimed Rheingold was the largest-selling brand in the East. AUTHOR COLLECTION

Miss Rheingold steps out for a night at the bowling alley in an outfit by Kinze of New York. In 1956, beer and bowling were an essential cornerstone of American leisure time. AUTHOR COLLECTION

Although the Rheingold Girl campaign wasn't an overnight sensation, it eventually became a hit with consumers. Jinx Falkenburg's face appeared on advertisement materials and packaging. Her face and the campaign were every advertising executive's dream come true. Rheingold was suddenly the brand in New York City.

As Miss Falkenburg's reign came to an end, Philip Liebmann and the Einson agency decided to have the Rheingold retail accounts choose a Rheingold Girl for 1941. The retailers didn't want to change and asked Liebmann to retain Jinx Falkenburg as the Rheingold spokesmodel. Philip Liebmann vetoed this notion and argued he wanted to keep the concept fresh. Liebmann looked at two dozen models and selected Ruth Ownbey.

Toward the end of 1941, the selection process was further refined. It was decided that the Rheingold Girl should be voted upon by a panel of six Rheingold executives and that she should be known as Miss Rheingold. Nancy Drake was the first Miss Rheingold chosen by popular vote. The same process continued for more than two decades.

The selection of Miss Rheingold was a major phenomenon in the five boroughs and beyond. She was the talk of the town and her face was everywhere. Her crowning was even discussed on street corners and in cartoons in the *New Yorker*.

Nancy Drake became Miss Rheingold 1942 in an election in which 200,000 votes were cast, and by the late 1940s, the number of votes reached into the millions. During the 1950s, the count exceeded 15 million annually, which was more than the votes cast in general elections. In 1952, 25 million votes were cast in the election of Mary Austin as Miss Rheingold 1953. This was about a dozen times more votes cast in New York City that year for Dwight Eisenhower and Adlai Stevenson, the major candidates in the presidential election.

The selection process that picked the half-dozen finalists each year received as much attention as the Miss America contest. The lavish program was held for many years at New York City's glamorous and expensive Waldorf Astoria Hotel and featured celebrity judges that included movies stars from Joan Fontaine to Douglas Fairbanks Jr., Casey Stengel of the New York Yankees, and Polly Bergen, a former Miss

Nancy Woodruff cuddles a dalmatian at New York City's Washington Square as a hook-and-ladder company stands by near the square's famous arch. By 1955, the posh Bergdorf Goodman store provided the costumes for Miss Rheingold.
AUTHOR COLLECTION

"Come and get it," says Hillie Merritt after cooking up a bunch of barbecued chicken and corn on the cob. In her summer frock by Bernard Newman, she looks fabulous for all her work over the barbecue.
AUTHOR COLLECTION

Nathalie "Tippi" Hedren was arguably the most famous Miss Rheingold finalist who didn't make the cut. She was a professional model and went on to television commercials after she competed for the 1954 title. Director Alfred Hitchcock spotted her on a commercial set in 1957, and she quickly became one of his favorite leading ladies. She is seen here with a friend in a promo for Hitchcock's **The Birds** (1963).
AUTHOR COLLECTION

The Miss Rheingolds

Hillie Merritt places the White Elephant headpiece on Bromley Stone at the 17th Annual White Elephant Party at the Ambassador Hotel. This January 1956 soiree was typical of the numerous public events attended by Miss Rheingold. AUTHOR COLLECTION

America. Invitations went out to a host of potential candidates, including every registered model in New York City. The day-long selection process was a major media event, and reporters and broadcast crews came to rub shoulders with the young women.

Many women competed in the annual event at the Waldorf, and six were chosen for the final round of public voting. The rest went home discouraged. In 1948, one 19-year-old, rejected from the final six, boarded the train for Philadelphia determined not to let it keep her down. Like many young women of her age, she had big dreams. Turned down by Rheingold, she decided to try Hollywood. It was a good thing she didn't give up. Her name was Grace Kelly.

Of course, some were lucky enough to make the final cut for two years.

In 1957, the six candidates for Miss Rheingold 1958 made the trip out to the Republic Aviation facility in Farmingdale on Long Island. Here, they posed for a series of photographs with Republic's first F105B Thunderchief. From the top, the contestants are Marylu Miner, Jolene Brand, Robbin Bain, Cathy Monahan, Madelyn Darrow, and Carolyn Stroupe. Madelyn Darrow was named Miss Rheingold 1958, and Rheingold fans had not seen the last of Robbin Bain. AUTHOR COLLECTION

In her role as Miss Rheingold 1958, Madelyn Darrow signs autographs for fans at a trade show in the New York Coliseum in November of that year. Her fan base among women was substantial. AUTHOR COLLECTION

Ann Hogan, Miss Rheingold 1952, had been a runner-up in 1951. Nancy Woodruff, Miss Rheingold 1955, was a runner-up two years earlier. Robbin Bain (sometimes listed as Robin Bain), Miss Rheingold 1959, was runner-up in 1958. Emily Banks, a runner-up in 1959, became Miss Rheingold 1960.

Although the faces changed, the slogan remained constant. Each Miss Rheingold attested to the fact that "My beer is Rheingold, the dry beer!" This placed Rainier four

decades ahead of the dry beer marketing scheme, a gimmick that had all of the major American and Canadian brewing companies competing for shelf space in the late 1980s.

By the mid-1950s, as Liebmann expanded its marketing and began brewing in California, the selection process for Miss Rheingold expanded. Miss Rheingold "primary elections" were held in Boston, Los Angeles, and New York City.

The beer business was also good for Rheingold. By 1956, it

was the largest-selling brand in the East. Two years later, Rheingold went abroad and brought home gold medals from the International Food and Beverage Exposition in Munich, and the 1958 Brussels World's Fair.

Most of the Miss Rheingolds and their runners-up melted back into relative obscurity after their year of fame. However, several continued in show business and a few achieved stardom. Jinx Falkenburg went on to appear in a total of more than a dozen feature films, including *Two Latins from Manhattan* (1941), *Sweetheart of the Fleet* (1942), *Two Señoritas from Chicago* (1943), *Talk About a Lady* (1946), and

This menu insert, featuring Madelyn Darrow, is typical of the advertising collateral material that Liebmann Brewing produced through the years to capitalize on the immense popularity of the reigning Miss Rheingold. AUTHOR COLLECTION

Madelyn Darrow takes to the court for a bit of doubles action. Whereas the Rheingold advertising of 1956 identified the brand as the top-selling beer in the East, the 1958 advertising noted that it was the largest-selling beer in New York. AUTHOR COLLECTION

This pheasant hunter is certainly more interested in Robbin Bain than hunting. One can imagine a couple of game birds roasting over an open fire, a couple of dogs, some cold Rheingold, and lively banter with Miss Rheingold. AUTHOR COLLECTION

Emily Banks confers with Rheingold chief Philip Liebmann at the Park Lane Hotel in New York City on December 15, 1959. Emily is basking in the glow of having just been elected Miss Rheingold 1960. *AUTHOR COLLECTION*

A runner-up in 1958, Robbin Bain was elected Miss Rheingold 1959. Here she is with a group of playful Rheingold sales managers at the annual November trade show at the New York Coliseum. *AUTHOR COLLECTION*

Emily Banks, the reigning Miss Rheingold 1960, reviews photographs of the slate of candidates for Miss Rheingold 1961. The finalists included Linda Bromley, Annette Cash, Liz Gardner, Peggy Jacobsen, and Barbara Weingarth. Janet Mick won the title. *AUTHOR COLLECTION*

Robbin Bain, Miss Rheingold 1959, makes a publicity appearance aboard the luxury liner Queen Elizabeth with brewery chief executive Philip Liebmann and an admirer. *AUTHOR COLLECTION*

Philip Liebmann enjoyed the merchandising aspect of his job as Rheingold's chief executive, and that included new products. Here, he and Janet Mick, Miss Rheingold 1961, are at the launch of the brewery's Golden Bock. Once a staple in the product lineup with most American breweries, bock beer was a rarity by the 1960s. AUTHOR COLLECTION

Meet Me on Broadway (1946). She married John Reagan "Tex" McCrary, and the two starred in the popular *Tex and Jinx* radio and television series for many years.

Ruth Ownbey had a bit part in *Du Barry Was a Lady* (1943), starring Red Skelton and Lucille Ball. Susann Shaw and Francine Counihan, runners-up in the 1943 and 1945 contests, each had cameos as cover girls in *Cover Girl* (1944), which starred Rita Hayworth. Rosemary Colligan, a runner-up for 1950, appeared in *Run for the Hills* (1953) and *The French Line* (1954). Miss Rheingold 1958, Madelyn Darrow, had a couple of bit parts in Hollywood but is best remembered as the wife of tennis star Pancho Gonzalez.

Emily Banks, Miss Rheingold 1960, had a career in television. She appeared in series such as *Wild Wild West* (1965), *Mannix* (1967), *Love, American Style* (1969), and *Highway to Heaven* (1984). She also was Yeoman Tonia Barrows in an episode of *Star Trek* in 1966. Carol Merrill, a runner-up for Miss Rheingold 1963, was a regular on the television game show *Let's Make a Deal*, which ran from 1963 to 1977.

Two runners-up who had especially important screen careers were Hope Lange and Nathalie "Tippi" Hedren, who competed, respectively, for the 1953 and 1954 Miss Rheingold titles. Lange grew up in New York City, where her father was an arranger for the Ziegfeld Follies. She made her Broadway debut at the age of 12 and ran for Miss Rheingold

at age 21. She became a star in her first film *Bus Stop* (1956) and had a supporting role to Marilyn Monroe. Lange's second film, *Peyton Place* (1957), earned an Academy Award nomination. She appeared opposite Elvis Presley in *Wild in the Country* (1961).

Tippi Hedren was discovered by Alfred Hitchcock in 1957 while filming a television commercial in New York City. He

Paul Hesse took this famous picture of Robbin Bain, Miss Rheingold 1959, greeting her successor, Emily Banks, at New York City's Idlewild International Airport. By this time, each Miss Rheingold made appearances on both coasts. This was facilitated by TransWorld Airlines' transcontinental jetliner service with Boeing 707s that began early in 1959. AUTHOR COLLECTION

cast her in *The Birds* (1963) and in the title role in *Marnie* (1964). She went on to appear in more than three dozen additional films and still acts today. Her daughter, Melanie Griffith, is also an actress.

The fortunes of Rheingold, like all of New York City's major brewers, faded in the early 1960s under the onslaught of the major national brands. This, along with the enormous cost of the acquisition and short-lived operation of the California breweries, compelled Liebmann Breweries to downsize. The site on Third Avenue was closed in 1961, and Pepsi Cola United Bottlers purchased Liebmann Breweries in 1964. The original Brooklyn plant and the New Jersey facility continued to operate under the Rheingold Breweries name.

With this turn of events, the decision was made to terminate the popular Miss Rheingold dynasty. Celeste Yarnall, Miss Rheingold 1964, was the last Miss Rheingold selected by the public. She went on to a successful Hollywood career. She appeared with Paul Newman in *A New Kind of Love* (1963), had the title role in the cult classic *The Face of Eve* (1968), and starred opposite Elvis Presley in *Live a Little, Love a Little*. Her film and television career extended beyond the turn of the century, but in recent years she is best known for her books on holistic medical care for domestic animals. She has a PhD in nutrition and was a professor of nutrition at Pacific Western University.

Striking a pose more like that of a twenty-first-century Miss Rheingold than of her predecessors, Celeste Yarnall held the title in 1964. She was the second-to-last Miss Rheingold of the twentieth century. As an actress, she later starred opposite Elvis Presley in Live a Little, Love a Little. *Elvis sang his legendary song "A Little Less Conversation" to Celeste. She was chosen as the Most Photogenic Beauty at the Cannes Film Festival.* AUTHOR COLLECTION

By the dawn of the twenty-first century, Rheingold was back in establishments across New York City. The packaging was now in clear glass, but the lettering on the new label design was classic Rheingold. COURTESY OF TERRY LIEBMAN, RHEINGOLD BREWING COMPANY

Kate Duyn was crowned in March 2003 as the first Miss Rheingold of the twenty-first century. Duyn grew up on the West Coast and came to New York City to pursue a career as a dancer and producer. When selected as Miss Rheingold, she was a bartender on the Lower East Side of Manhattan.
COURTESY OF TERRY LIEBMAN, RHEINGOLD BREWING COMPANY

Sharon Vaughn, Miss Rheingold 1965, was the last Miss Rheingold. She was selected by brewery executives, rather than elected by the public.

Rheingold Breweries continued to operate under the new ownership for about another decade and was dogged by the slumping sales that often accompanies the sale of a family-owned firm to outside interests. The original Brooklyn brewery closed in 1976, and the New Jersey brewery closed the following year.

Two decades later, Rheingold returned. In 1997, Mike Mitaro left his job as a marketing manager with Labatt United States, founded the Rheingold Brewing Company, and revived the legendary brand. The new Rheingold beer was brewed from an original Rheingold recipe at the F. X. Matt Brewing Company in Utica, New York.

Mitaro's extensive career in marketing management included working at the Stroh Brewery Company. Walter "Terry" Liebman (who spells his name with one *n*), a member of the original Liebmann family, was selected as chairman of the board. Terry Liebman had worked in marketing at the original Liebmann Breweries until 1961, when he left to work in the brokerage and investment banking industry.

Mitaro left after a few years, and the new CEO and president of the new company was Tom Bendheim, who had extensive experience in consumer marketing and management,

including five years as CEO at Dooney and Bourke. He was related to the Liebmann family by marriage.

Early in 2003, the Rheingold Brewing Company brought back Miss Rheingold. Whereas the original Miss Rheingolds were selected from a pool of models and actresses, the twenty-first century Miss Rheingolds were chosen from bartenders and waitresses in the New York City area.

On March 10, 2003, Kate Duyn was crowned Miss Rheingold 2003 at a spirited event held at the Ukrainian National Home. Loretta Rissell, Miss Rheingold 1963, attended the festivities. Originally from Portland, Oregon, Duyn lived and worked on the Lower East Side of Manhattan.

Later in 2003, the Rheingold Brewing Company allowed the public to choose Miss Rheingold 2004, and technology permitted Rheingold fans to vote online at the Rheingold

Loretta Rissell (Miss Rheingold of 1963), Francine Counihan (a Miss Rheingold finalist in 1945), and Rheingold CEO Tom Bendheim are pictured with Kate Duyn as she was crowned Miss Rheingold on March 10, 2003. COURTESY OF TERRY LIEBMAN, RHEINGOLD BREWING COMPANY

This card was the back stop of the ballot box for the 2004 Miss Rheingold contest. Dani Marco, upper right, was the winner. The runners-up included Erin Bailey of Carroll Gardens, Kim Barbakoff of Uniondale, Raquel Flecha from Sheepshead Bay, Carmel Macklin who worked in Midtown Manhattan, and Shequida, who worked on the Upper East Side of Manhattan. *COURTESY OF TERRY LIEBMAN, RHEINGOLD BREWING COMPANY*

Brewing Company website. In November 2003, Dani Marco was selected as Miss Rheingold 2004.

In a town where start-up breweries come and go with fearsome frequency, Rheingold was a start-up brewery that started up with not only a name that was ingrained into the New York City cultural landscape, but a tradition that was arguably the most important aspect of beer culture in the entire history of New York City.

Dani Marco was an aspiring actress and a bartender at the 13 Little Devils on Orchard Street in Manhattan's Lower East Side when she was elected Miss Rheingold 2004. COURTESY OF TERRY LIEBMAN, RHEINGOLD BREWING COMPANY

This is the classic Schlitz label as it appeared after the Milwaukee brewery closed in 1982. The label design was essentially the same as it had been for more than 42 years, but the tagline changed from "the Beer That Made Milwaukee Famous," to simply "A Great American Beer since 1849." *AUTHOR COLLECTION*

CHAPTER 12

Schlitz

MILWAUKEE WAS TO American brewing what Detroit was to the auto industry, or what Hollywood was to motion pictures. Milwaukee was beer, and Schlitz was "the Beer That Made Milwaukee Famous." How it accomplished this, especially in the company of many of the greatest names in American brewing, is a testament to the foresight of the company's namesake and founder.

This is the sprawling Schlitz Brewing Company facility in Milwaukee as it appeared around the turn of the twentieth century. The massive seven-story brew house is located immediately behind the red-roofed headquarters building. *AUTHOR COLLECTION*

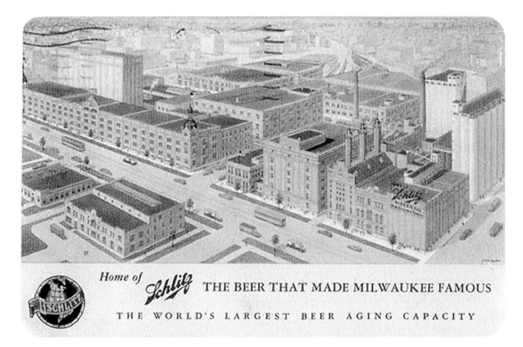

Home of *Schlitz* THE BEER THAT MADE MILWAUKEE FAMOUS
THE WORLD'S LARGEST BEER AGING CAPACITY

Born in Germany, Joseph Schlitz arrived in Milwaukee in 1850 and worked as a brewer for August Krug. When Krug died in 1856, Schlitz took over the company and married Krug's widow. Schlitz died in 1875. He made Milwaukee famous with the brand that bore his name. *BILL YENNE*

Joseph Schlitz was born in Mainz in the German state of Hesse and came to Milwaukee in 1850 at the age of 20. There, Schlitz went to work for August Krug, a recent German immigrant who started a brewery in 1849 on Chestnut Street across the street from the early lager breweries of David Gipfel and Jacob Best, the forerunner of the great Pabst empire.

When Krug died in 1856, Schlitz took over management of the company. Two years later, Schlitz married Anna Krug, August's widow, and renamed the company Joseph Schlitz Brewing.

In the early 1870s, Schlitz began construction of the large brewery facility at Third and Walnut streets that formed the centerpiece of the Schlitz empire for the next century. Beneath the site, Schlitz drilled for more than a thousand feet to tap a half-dozen artesian wells. At the time, much of the water used in Milwaukee breweries was pumped from Lake Michigan or the Menominee River.

How the Schlitz brand made Milwaukee famous is an amazing story that might have served to inspire a heroic novel. In the middle of the nineteenth century, Milwaukee hadn't secured its position as the brewing capital of America or the region. Its chief rival was Chicago, a much larger city situated on America's great railway crossroads. Then came the Great Chicago Fire of 1871.

The windy city was decimated in this monumental fire, and along with thousands of other structures, most of the great Chicago breweries were

Although the beer was known informally as such since 1871, the Joseph Schlitz Brewing Company didn't officially adopt the slogan "the Beer That Made Milwaukee Famous" until 1893. AUTHOR COLLECTION

destroyed. The city laid waste and was out of beer. The rebuilding effort required an immense amount of materials, and the workers doing the rebuilding required beer.

Joseph Schlitz led the effort to get emergency supplies of beer into the ruined city. Other Milwaukee brewers became involved in this essential relief effort, but the people of Chicago saw and remembered the Schlitz brand name. It was a charitable act that turned into a public relations coup.

The Great Fire made Schlitz famous, but Schlitz made Milwaukee and its brewing industry famous. The Chicago brewing industry never fully recovered its former glory, and Milwaukee became the capital of American brewing. Although Schlitz was known as the beer that had put Milwaukee brewing on the map, the greatest slogan in American brewing

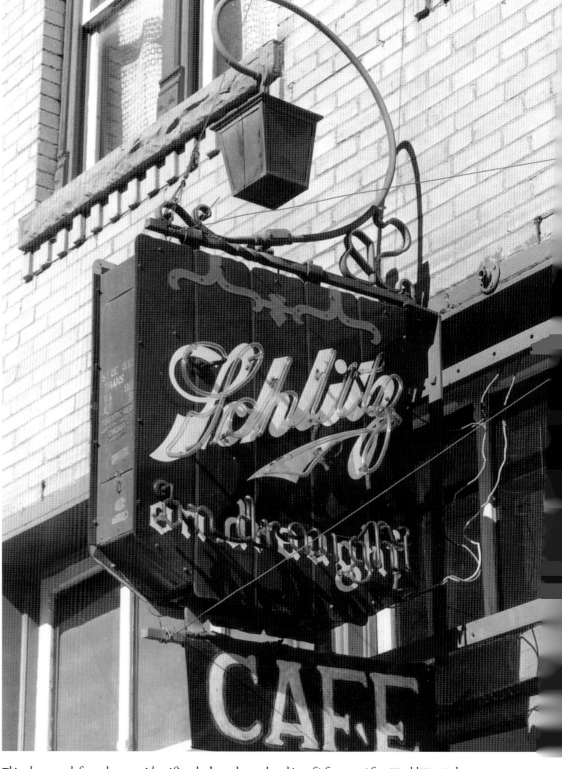

This photograph from the 1930s identifies the beer that makes this café famous. After World War II the term draft *replaced the English variation* draught *when referring to beer served from kegs in the United States. AUTHOR COLLECTION*

history wasn't officially adopted and used in advertising for more than two decades.

Schlitz emerged from the pack and became Milwaukee's number two brewer behind Pabst. In 1874, Schlitz Brewing produced nearly 70,000 barrels, which was up from 50,000 barrels the year before.

In 1875, Joseph Schlitz decided to make a trip back to Germany to visit relatives. Their successful businessman cousin from America never arrived. The steamship he was on, the SS *Schiller*, ran aground off Britain's Land's End and Schlitz drowned. Widowed a second time, Anna lived until 1887.

Joseph's death saw the management and control of Joseph Schlitz Brewing passed to August Uihlein and his brothers, Henry, Edward, and Alfred. August had befriended the Krug family as a child, and Schlitz hired the 16-year-old Uihlein as a bookkeeper in 1858. Uihlein worked in St. Louis from 1860 to 1868, but returned to the Schlitz company and worked his way up the corporate ladder. He had been the point man for Schlitz when he went to Chicago after the fire.

Beginning in 1935, many major brewing companies in the United States canned their beer. Working with the Continental Can Company, Schlitz was the first to use the cone-top cans that simulated the look and feel of a bottle. COURTESY OF THE DAN AUGUSTINER COLLECTION

By 1940, Schlitz scrapped the brown label and used the cream, brown, and gold label that remained the standard for many decades to come. This elegant ad positioned the brand as a stylish beverage. Schlitz became the first American brewer to package beer in brown bottles in 1912. Before that time, beer was bottled in clear glass, through which sunlight can damage the quality of the beer. Even today, many brewers still use clear glass bottles. AUTHOR COLLECTION

Having introduced its cone-top cans in 1935, Schlitz reintroduced the easy-to-carry, short-necked Steinie bottle in 1937. It was described as being "remindful of olden days" and likely to take less space in your refrigerator. The contents were, however, the "same as [the] regular bottle." AUTHOR COLLECTION

The Beer That Made Milwaukee Famous

Today...It's Schlitz in "Steinies"

TASTE SCHLITZ TODAY... in the new, compact, easy-to-handle "Steinie" Brown Bottle. It is remindful of olden days . . . of beer sipped from the cool depths of stone steins.

Old-time brewmasters never enjoyed the facilities of modern science to assure uniform deliciousness to their brew but Schlitz has expended millions of dollars in research and development to make each glass uniformly delicious, appetizing and healthful.

With the first sip you instantly recognize the difference between Schlitz and other beers. That delightful, satisfying difference is old-time flavor which Schlitz brews with scientific uniformity into every sparkling drop.

It's the full-bodied flavor of rich barley-malt wedded to the piquant tang of the finest hops the world affords... brewed to the peak of ripe, mellow perfection under Schlitz Precise Enzyme Control. You may choose from the modern "Steinie" Brown Bottle . . . tall Brown Bottle . . . or Cap-Sealed Can . . . whichever suits your needs. Each brings you Schlitz at its best.

Schlitz "Steinie" Brown Bottles are compact—light in weight—easy to carry—take less space in your refrigerator. Contents same as regular bottle.

Copyright 1937, Jos. Schlitz Brewing

JOS. SCHLITZ BREWING CO. Milwaukee, Wis.

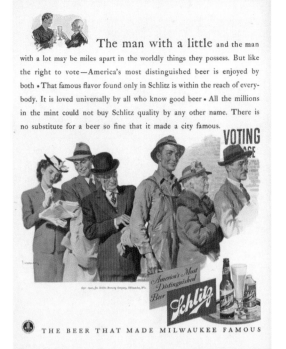

August Uihlein managed the company for 36 years—longer than Schlitz himself—until his death in 1911. During these years, Joseph Schlitz Brewing solidified its position as the number two brewer in Milwaukee behind, but never far behind, Pabst. Schlitz was always in the top five nationally. In 1879, under Uihlein, Schlitz Brewing produced 110,832 barrels to Pabst's 180,152 barrels.

Uihlein began mass-bottling Schlitz beer in Milwaukee in 1877 and was also very aggressive and expanded the number of brewery-owned saloons, taverns, and beer gardens that Schlitz operated in Milwaukee, Chicago, and elsewhere. The company also owned and operated Schlitz Hotels in Milwaukee; Winona, Minnesota; and Omaha, Nebraska. Schlitz Park, with its bandstand and carousel, was a center of civic life in Milwaukee. A Schlitz bottling plant in Cleveland, Ohio, opened in 1883, and the annual output from the Schlitz brewery in Milwaukee topped half a million barrels in 1886.

In 1893, August Uihlein formally adopted the slogan "the Beer That Made Milwaukee Famous" for use in the company's advertising. Five years later, during the Spanish American War, Admiral Dewey achieved his dramatic victory in the Battle of Manila Bay. To celebrate, Uihlein sent a shipload of Schlitz to the American service personnel in the Philippines. As in Chicago a quarter-century earlier, the gesture was a public relations coup.

The prominence of the Schlitz slogan at the turn of the century is evident in its ability to inspire parodies. When the beer from the tiny Heger Brewing Company in Jefferson, Wisconsin, happened to beat Schlitz in an exposition

The numerous important graphic elements in this 1942 Schlitz advertising piece tell many stories about the company at mid-twentieth century. First of all, there are excellent illustrations of the Schlitz-invented cone-top can and a Schlitz bottle. Next, it tells a great deal about the light, lager nature of the beer by the color in the glass and about the healthy fermentation by the smooth, not soapy, character of the head. Then, of course, there is an excellent bird's-eye view of the brewery and the Menominee River snaking through Milwaukee. Finally, there is an early view of the woman with the "kiss of the hops" slogan that dominated Schlitz advertising through the coming years. The idea was that women did not like bitter beer. AUTHOR COLLECTION

IT MADE A *City* FAMOUS

Mention Milwaukee anywhere in the world and people say, "That's where they make Schlitz, the beer that made Milwaukee famous." To earn a reputation for having made a city famous is an achievement of which any product may be proud. Almost a century ago people began telling each other about the fine beer produced by SCHLITZ

in Milwaukee. As the fame of this great brew spread, so did the name of its home town—Milwaukee became synonymous with Schlitz. Today, that same fine quality has earned further honors. Everywhere Schlitz is referred to as *America's most distinguished beer*. Discover the reason for yourself. Just taste this marvelous beer and you'll never want to go back to a bitter beer—you'll always demand SCHLITZ.

The young woman is planning an elegant soirée, and a discerning hostess knows that "gracious hospitality calls for the best." By 1946, Schlitz had learned that women defined the "best" as beer that had no harsh bitterness. Unfortunately, by reducing the hops, Schlitz charted the course toward blandness. A generation later, the "kiss of hops" strategy turned out to be a kiss of another kind. AUTHOR COLLECTION

taste test, the upstart coined the rival slogan "the Beer That Made Milwaukee Jealous."

Although Pabst had the distinction of being the largest brewing company in the United States at the turn of the twentieth century, the Joseph Schlitz Brewing Company was close on its heels. Annual sales of Schlitz exceeded a million barrels and finally topped those of Pabst for the first time in 1902.

As seen in the Chicago example, Schlitz recognized the importance of mass distribution of its beer. The company was a pioneer in multisite brewing. In 1908, Schlitz built a satellite brewery in Cleveland, Ohio, from scratch.

When Henry Uihlein took over management of the company in 1911, the American brewing industry faced the growing power of the temperance movement. Nine years later, the 18th Amendment imposed Prohibition on the United States. Schlitz hoped to make the city famous with a near-beer called Famo. The company had the foresight to introduce this nonalcoholic product in 1917 in anticipation of Prohibition.

Not all of the company's Prohibition-era ventures succeeded. Schlitz reportedly lost several million dollars manufacturing the Eline brand of chocolate products. Until the 21st Amendment ended Prohibition in 1933, the company used the slogan "Schlitz, the Name That Made Milwaukee Famous," but quickly resurrected the old phrase after the repeal.

By 1934, Schlitz was back to a million-barrel annual output. The following year, advances in packaging led brewers to canned beer. Krueger Brewing of Newark was the first to can beer and used a flat-topped can in the shape of a modern beer can. Schlitz soon followed suit with a cone-top can that was developed by the Continental Can Company and was shaped like a bottle.

By World War II, Schlitz was solidly in the lead as the largest brewing company in the United States. In 1950, the company had an annual output of 5.1 million barrels, compared to 4.9 million barrels for second-place Anheuser-Busch. Together, the two companies accounted for 12 percent of the beer sold in the United States.

These figures soon grew thanks to a huge expansion undertaken by the two industry leaders after the end of World War II. These two giants from the middle of the country moved to establish themselves as national brewers and built massive state-of-the-art breweries on both coasts.

"Now watch him drop that paper!"

The Beer that made Milwaukee Famous

This young wife has found the key to getting her man's attention. In this 1948 ad, Schlitz has omitted the "kiss of hops" tagline. AUTHOR COLLECTION

Schlitz leapt ahead when it bought the George Ehret Brewery on George Street in Brooklyn in 1949. This brewery is historically important and was a satellite operation for the Manhattan brewery that was the largest in the United States during the later nineteenth century before

Before Prohibition, the schooners ordered in taverns were 32 ounces and sold for a nickel. When they returned after Prohibition, they still sold for a nickel, albeit not for long, and contained half as much beer. Schooners remained the standard tavern glass in the United States through the 1940s and 1950s.
BILL YENNE

Milwaukee emerged as the nation's brewing capital. The Brooklyn facility dated back to a brewery founded on the site in 1866 by Hubert Fischer and Leonhard Eppig. It had been owned by the Ehret company for 14 years when Schlitz acquired it.

Anheuser-Busch built a new plant in Newark, New Jersey, which opened in 1951.

In 1954, the two competitors became the first major brewing companies with coast to coast networks of breweries, and they both opened new facilities in the Los Angeles area. The Schlitz plant was constructed on Woodman Avenue in the fast-growing suburb of Van Nuys in the San Fernando Valley. Schlitz made its next move in 1956 and acquired the former Muehleback Brewery in Kansas City, Missouri—

"I was curious...

I tasted it...

Now I know *why* Schlitz is...

The Beer that made Milwaukee Famous!"

© 1949, JOS. SCHLITZ BREWING CO., MILWAUKEE, WIS.

61

Anheuser-Busch's back yard. The rivalry between the two companies was a bitter one.

In 1959, both of the national giants opened facilities in Tampa, Florida, but Anheuser-Busch replaced Schlitz as America's leading brewer. In 1960, Anheuser-Busch had an annual output of 8.5 million barrels compared to 5.7 million for Schlitz and 4.9 million for third-place Falstaff. Together, the three industry leaders cornered nearly a quarter of the American beer market. The age of the great and powerful national brewers had arrived.

During the coming decade, Schlitz expanded into the South with new breweries at Longview, Texas, in 1966; Winston-Salem, North Carolina, in 1970; and Memphis, Tennessee, in 1971.

In 1956, Schlitz was beer that stylish young people took on picnics to the beach. The advertising copy still whispered the "kiss of hops" message and promised that Schlitz was "never, never filling (even with charcoal-broiled steaks!)." AUTHOR COLLECTION

Fresh from the trout stream, a perky young woman sits down in this 1961 ad to enjoy a pilsner glass of the beer that "always tastes alive." Schlitz insists that she's looking for a beer with "just the kiss of hops." AUTHOR COLLECTION

In 1962, Schlitz promoted its product as having "real gusto," although it added the caveat that it was a light beer. In any case, the man with the schooner seems pleased with the taste. A "kiss of hops" would probably not have been what he wanted. AUTHOR COLLECTION

Schlitz acquired the Burgermeister Brewing Company of San Francisco in 1963. Adding Burgie to the Schlitz portfolio boosted sales nearly 20 percent. Ironically, the Burgermeister facility, which was started in San Francisco in 1868, was known as the Milwaukee Brewery from 1880 until Prohibition. Schlitz sold it to Meisterbrau of Chicago in 1969, and it was part of the Falstaff portfolio from 1971 to 1978.

Another addition to the product line in 1963 was Schlitz Malt Liquor, a high-alcohol lager. The term *malt liquor* was a legal requirement because of the high alcohol content of this particular lager. Contrary to the popular myth, there is no such style of beer as malt liquor. The label of this new product pictured a bull that was based on a photograph of Prince, Henry Uihlein's prize bull.

While Schlitz continued to be marketed as the Beer That Made Milwaukee Famous, its advertising people toyed with a number of other secondary slogans. During the 1940s, when it was the largest-selling brand in the United States, Schlitz

had been consistently advertised as "America's most distinguished beer." During the 1960s, the term "Gusto" was worked into a number of print ads and television commercials. The phrase "When you're out of Schlitz, you're out of beer" was introduced in 1966 and used in print and broadcast advertising.

In 1964, Schlitz acquired the Hawaii Brewing Company, located on Kamehameha Highway in Honolulu. The company was founded just after Prohibition and its Primo Beer had a loyal cult following throughout the islands. Schlitz continued brewing Primo in Hawaii until 1979, but attempts to keep up the mystique after production moved to the mainland was unsuccessful.

Other Schlitz acquisitions during the late 1960s ranged from shares in breweries in Europe and the Caribbean to California's Geyser Peak winery. Meanwhile, the company curtailed other operations. In 1973, as total beer production at Schlitz reached 21.3 million barrels, the company moved to

By 1963, brewing companies were ready to banish the church key to the dusty shelves of history. The pull tab idea was introduced around 1962 and was soon used everywhere. Of course, the blizzard of discarded tabs led to refinement of the concept. AUTHOR COLLECTION

Be glad you're thirsty. Schlitz drinks down light and cool. Tastes great, even after your thirst is gone. Schlitz. The beer that made Milwaukee famous simply because it tastes so good. Now in the Pop Top—the can with the built in opener!

real gusto
in a great light beer

There is real gusto on the concert stage, as the cellist sips a mug of Schlitz, circa 1964. AUTHOR COLLECTION

How do you follow an act like this? With another Schlitz. Light, but all gusto. Encore? You bet!

real gusto
in a great light beer
Schlitz

Real gusto is at the ballpark, as the young man happily serves up some cups of Schlitz, circa 1963. The product was described as having "beer-y vigor." Schlitz said that "Brewmasters call it character. We call it 'gusto.'" Webster describes gusto as either "individual taste" or "vigorous enjoyment." AUTHOR COLLECTION

real gusto
in a great light beer

Almost anyone can make light beer. But it takes a lot of doing (and just the kiss of the hops) to give a light brew all the beer-y vigor it should have. Brewmasters call it character. We call it "gusto." And in Schlitz you get it in spades.

The Beer that made Milwaukee Famous . . . simply because it tastes so good. Schlitz...ahhh!

Schlitz

By 1964, Schlitz advertising was long on gusto, but short on verbiage. This man prepares to quaff a yard of light lager. I certainly wouldn't recommend doing this in a nice shirt, unless you've had some practice. AUTHOR COLLECTION

By 1966, Schlitz had consigned its gusto advertising campaign to history and adopted the brand's last major slogan, "When you're out of Schlitz, you're out of beer." However, the generation coming of age in the ensuing decade no longer thought of the brand as the definitive beer. AUTHOR COLLECTION

consolidate its holdings and closed the Kansas City and Brooklyn breweries. The latter was taken offline in anticipation of a new plant that Schlitz planned to build upstate near Baldwinsville, New York. When it was finished in 1977, its 5.8 million barrel capacity made it the largest plant ever operated by the company. While it was being built, the company's East Coast production was consolidated at the North Carolina facility.

By this time, the fortunes of Milwaukee's leading company began to fall. The catalyst for the downfall of Schlitz Brewing came in 1976, when millions of bottles of beer produced at the Memphis and Tampa breweries went bad. The image of these being destroyed was a public relations disaster. At the same time, Schlitz reformulated its already pale lager to be even lighter. The company may have been able to cut production costs by doing this, but the public perception was that Schlitz was also cutting the quality of the beer. Even as the company invested in a nationwide plant modernization program, sales were declining.

An event symbolic of the times for Schlitz came in 1979, with the sale of its two-year-old Baldwinsville brewery to rival Anheuser-Busch.

Primo Beer was probably the most popular locally produced beer in the history of Hawaii when Schlitz bought the brand in 1964. The Milwaukee icon rode the wave of Primo's success like Duke Kahanamoku riding a big one at Waimea until 1979, when Schlitz made the unfathomable corporate decision to stop brewing Primo in the islands. BILL YENNE

By 1981, Schlitz was on the ropes and entertained buyout offers from Pabst and G. Heileman. The latter won the bidding, but the deal was nixed by the U.S. Justice Department on antitrust grounds. A year later, the Stroh Brewing Company of Detroit made an offer that pleased the feds.

In March 1982, the brewer that brewed the beer that made Milwaukee famous was sold to a brewer from Detroit, who closed the Schlitz plant in Milwaukee. In a further twist of irony, Stroh closed its own Detroit flagship brewery in 1985 and concentrated production at the former Schlitz facilities, notably in Winston-Salem and Tampa.

As the former Schlitz brewery complex in Milwaukee was remodeled as an office park, the Schlitz brand continued to be marketed by Stroh until 1999, when the company was sold to Pabst.

Schlitz and Pabst, the two old Milwaukee rivals, who had grown up within shouting distance from one another, were now under the same roof, although that roof was now nearly a thousand miles away in San Antonio, Texas. Certainly neither Frederick Pabst nor Joseph Schlitz could have ever foreseen this twist of fate that played out in the final hours of the twentieth century.

Although Schlitz identified itself as a "great light beer since 1962," it was more than a decade before there was a Schlitz Light. This label was used between 1982, when Stroh Brewing bought the Schlitz brand, and 1985, when Stroh closed their flagship brewery in Detroit. AUTHOR COLLECTION

One of the popular products that slipped into the Stroh portfolio in 1982 was Schlitz Malt Liquor. The brand's well-known insignia was derived from an image of Prince, Henry Uihlein's prize bull. A Prince look-alike was used in some memorable television spots in the 1980s that featured him crashing the walls of bachelor pads. AUTHOR COLLECTION

Index